MW00987010

NATURE SPIRITS,
SPIRIT GUIDES,
AND GHOSTS

NATURE SPIRITS, SPIRIT GUIDES, AND GHOSTS

How to Talk with and Photograph Beings of Other Realms

ATALA DOROTHY TOY

QUEST
BOOKS

Theosophical Publishing House
Wheaton, Illinois * Chennai, India

Copyright © 2012 by Atala Dorothy Toy

First Quest Edition 2012

All rights reserved. No part of this book may be reproduced in any manner except for quotations embodied in critical articles or reviews. For additional information write to

Quest Books
Theosophical Publishing House
P. O. Box 270
Wheaton, IL 60187-0270

www.questbooks.net

Cover design by Greta Polo
Typesetting by Wordstop Technologies, Chennai, India
Photo credits:
Pages 17, 205 by Melanie J. France, page 18 by Lanette Padula. All other photos by Atala Dorothy Toy.

Library of Congress Cataloging-in-Publication Data

Toy, Atala Dorothy.

Nature spirits, spirit guides, and ghosts: how to talk with and photograph beings of other realms / Atala Dorothy Toy. —1st Quest ed.

    p.   cm.

Includes index.
ISBN 978-0-8356-0902-9
1. Spirits. 2. Spiritualism. 3. Spirit photography. 4. Spiritual life—Miscellanea.
I. Title.

BF1552. T69 2012
133.9—dc23   2011041871

5   4   3   2   *   12   13   14   15   16

Printed in the United States of America

This book is dedicated to nature lovers everywhere.

Table of Contents

List of Illustrations   ix

Introduction   1

Chapter 1 – Ghosts and Spirits   33

    A Visit from the Angel of Death   33

    Many Doors Lead to the Beyond   37

    The Ghost Who Washed Dishes   39

    Mafia Hit Man   45

    The Ghost Cat   48

    The Novena   50

    The Haunted Hotel   53

Chapter 2 – Humans, Spirit Guides, and Thought Forms   57

    Folds in Time   57

    Guardian of the Spring   73

    The Roundtable of the Heart   80

    Masonic Hauntings   96

    The Lady Who Lived in the Dark   98

    The Horse Who Knew More Than His Owners   106

    The Jilted House—Spirit of Place   111

Chapter 3 – Earth Energies   117

    Time Travel   117

    Portal Problems   124

    The Bog Orb   130

    A Faery's Worst Offense   135

    Portals to Other Worlds   137

    Sinkholes and Tree Meridians   141

Table of Contents

Negative and Positive Vortexes   147

Give Us Back Ganesh!   150

How Trees Hold Space   153

Chapter 4 – Rock, Tree, and Faery Spirits   **159**

Grandfather Rock   159

Moss Faeries—Maine   168

The Moss Faery—New Hampshire   175

The Stranded Gnome   183

The Owl on Turtle Island   186

The Balsam Who Loved the Birch   190

The Rock Elf and the Maiden/Crone   195

Grandmother Tree   198

The Heron, the Lizard, and the Green Faery   201

Epilogue – What Happens Next?   **207**

Notes   **211**

Index   **215**

About the Author   **225**

Illustrations

0.1.	The flower of life	8
0.2.	Star of David, Star tetrahedron, Mandala of creation	8
0.3.	Triangle	8
0.4.	Star tetrahedron	8
0.5.	The St. Michael line	14
0.6.	Multiple orbs	17
0.7.	Bear totem	18
0.8.	Burr oak bear totem	19
2.1.	Protected Native American village	62
2.2.	Marauders' camp	63
2.3.	Medicine man's vortex	63
2.4.	Medicine man's seat	64
2.5.	Trees in medicine man's focus	65
2.6.	Medicine man's circle of energy	65
2.7.	Tree in medicine man's energy circle	66
2.8.	Another thought form	67
2.9.	Thought form guardian	74
2.10.	Madame Blavatsky with Kuthumi, Morya, and St. Germain	88
2.11.	Bear face in redwood burl	95
3.1.	The magnolia portal	119
3.2.	Reverse view of grove	120
3.3.	Unstable portal	126
3.4.	Disturbed tree growth	127
3.5.	Sideways trees	127
3.6.	Colleagues identifying energy	128
3.7.	Hole in the ground	129
3.8.	The bog orb	131
3.9.	The heart portal	138

3.10.	Alpha trees with heart portal	139
3.11.	Collage of portals	140
3.12.	Sinkholes and trees	144
3.13.	Time collage of tree	154
3.14.	Space college of trees	155
4.1.	Grandfather rock	160
4.2.	Grandma and baby rock	161
4.3.	Bird family	161
4.4.	The elephant rock	162
4.5.	The bird warrior	162
4.6.	Abandoned altar	163
4.7.	Snake head altar	164
4.8.	Lichen heart	164
4.9.	Moss faery	177
4.10.	Close-up of moss faery	178
4.11.	Pixie looking down from tree apartment	182
4.12.	Pixie playing with twig	183
4.13.	Owl on turtle island	187
4.14.	Kissing balsam and birch trees	191
4.15.	Unfriendly balsam & birch	193
4.16.	The rock elf and the maiden/crone	196
4.17.	Detail of rock elf and maiden/crone	197
4.18.	Grandmother tree collage of space	199
4.19.	Bird head with frog eye	200
4.20.	Heron, lizard, faery	203
4.21.	Group of photographers	205

There is no one who knows you better than yourself.
Only you know what works for you and what doesn't.
Therefore, you should never let others' opinions define who you are.
—Buddha

Introduction

Faeries, angels, ghosts, orbs, and spirit of place are some of the real life forms who exist in distinct worlds that interrelate with our human realm.

We share the universe with a wide variety of life forms. Most of these life forms share similar motivations: the need to survive, thrive, prosper, protect themselves, assist others, grow in self-awareness, and learn to exist as solitary units and in cooperation with others. These life forms have a wide variety of motivations and behavior patterns within their worlds—also just like us.

This is a book of stories that can help you understand the sometimes strange experiences you may have when you feel something or someone is attempting to communicate with you, or is affecting you, but you don't know what it is or what to do about it. The book covers a fairly broad range of occurrences, for the stories are drawn not only from my experiences but from those of clients who have come to me for help. You can enjoy each story and then learn the principles involved in its resolution—principles you can apply to your own experiences. Some of the stories in this book include photographs of the life forms involved.

We all are communicating interdimensionally every day, but we may not realize it. So we lose out on many marvels of cooperation and ways to improve our lives—by learning, for instance, to watch before we leap or to receive help from conscious life forms who are sharing our common space. The interdimensional communicators know we are often affected by the actions of life forms cosharing our space, such as plants, animals, nature spirits, and angels.

As a professional interdimensional communicator, I am called upon to solve issues that affect a client's well-being. Sometimes the source of a problem is not observable to the client; the source could as easily be earth grids as an unhappy ghost.

Sometimes clients complain that the life forms they sense around them or on their property are dark and malevolent. When I discuss the matter with the life forms, I usually find that they have a specific objective or need that the human has been obstructing out of ignorance. Once the two forms—human and other—understand each other and are willing to cooperate, the situation is usually peacefully resolved.

Following each story there are one to three sections: a lesson that explains the energetic principles of the situation; an exercise to help you master the principle contained in the story; and photographs that offer tips so that you can photograph such life forms yourself.

If you would like to simply enjoy the stories and photographs and learn from them, please turn now to the first chapter. If you would like some technical background about how it is possible to communicate with life forms in other worlds, please continue reading this introduction to the process.

Energy can be experienced many ways. This book is based on the foundational understanding that, at its source, all energy is ultimately one. This one source has evolved over time into numerous specialized life forms, each of which developed in response to specific needs and experiences. In a universe of free will, every choice a life form makes, from the moment of their individuation from source, shapes the future path the life form will then proceed upon. As a life form exists over time, its myriad decisions, minor and large, eventually shape it into a unique expression of the one source. As energy evolves down through the frequencies—from light to liquid light to subtle form to solid form—life forms who are close to each other in energetic frequency, or consciousness, can see and interact with one another fairly easily. Life forms who may once have known each other, but who have evolved in radically different ways, often lose the ability to see and communicate with one another. It's like childhood friends who choose radically different lifestyles as they grow up and no longer have anything in common with each other.

Maturity of consciousness brings with it the ability to comprehend not only the divergent views of other humans but also the divergent life forms of other frequencies. Such understanding comes from the ability of a life form to identify with the one source, or with multiple aspects of the source, and to also identify with various modes of the source's manifestation. This is communication on an interdimensional level.

The adventures described in this book are not an exploration of the supernatural. They are part of the emerging field of spiritual sciences. To paraphrase the words of one of the Theosophical Society's founders, Madame Blavatsky, when asked to explain what "supernatural" powers were, she responded that there *is* no supernatural—there is only the natural, and that is super!

While mainstream Western philosophy, science, and religion have in recent centuries sought to disprove the existence of anything that could not be seen, touched, or heard, there have been many philosophies, sciences, and cultures that have accepted the reality of multiple divergent dimensions and the multifarious life forms who make up our universe.

Today, our world is growing into a greater understanding of frequency, resonance, and consciousness. With this growth comes an appreciation of the interconnectedness of the hard sciences, the soft sciences, and the metaphysical. Interworld communication is one of the emerging fields of spiritual sciences.

Because of current Western cultural taboos, when people sense something is around but unseen, they often attempt to shut out that awareness. They unconsciously feel this is safer than attempting to deal with the consequences of some life form being present. The only place Westerners feel safe in acknowledging these life forms is in fiction—books, movies, and video games. These media have provided us with a rich body of "fantastical" work, and many seers have expressed their knowledge in fictional form. By definition, fiction is a work of the imagination and therefore its reality does not have to meet scientific standards of proof. Therefore, as a culture we do not yet have a broad body of scientific information about interdimensional life forms; the West is culturally backward in this regard.

However, there are other cultures that acknowledge these life forms, and their stories tell of real contact with diverse beings, the life forms' functions, and how to work with them. Many of these cultures, which used to be considered "ignorant," "indigenous," "simplistic nature worshippers," "heathens," or "weird" are now understood by mainstream Western society to be extremely advanced in their ability to affect and change matter—just in a way far different from that of the Western "norm."

For example, dowsers—people who locate water, lost property, and lost children by moving a pendulum or rod over a map, person, or piece of land—understand very well that all existence is energy, that it moves in specific configurations such as lines and vortexes, and that humans can travel in consciousness along those lines, backward and forward in time and space, and accurately acquire information.

The many pagan traditions of the West and such Eastern traditions as Shintoism understand the live quality of all nature. Many indigenous New Zealand, Australian, and South American cultures have alternate ways to experience existence, as well as totally different understandings of the nature of time and interactions between worlds. The great occult traditions of the ancient Egyptians, the Kabbalists, the Greeks, the Hindus, Buddhists, and the Norse have each contributed significant information for understanding the energetic mechanics of our world and the universe.

Within all these vastly varied cultures, one finds highly evolved visionaries who understood their tradition's core energies as either, or both, living beings with whom they could communicate or flowing light fields who can coalesce into specific energies and then into specific forms.

To find in-depth information on these esoteric traditions, explore libraries and Quest bookstores affiliated with the Theosophical Society. The Society encourages open-minded inquiry to understand the wisdom of the ages, respect the unity of all life, and help people explore spiritual self-transformation. Their research material, bookstores, and events reflect their eclectic appreciation of all positive worldviews, and they provide a safe environment for personal explorations.

This book reflects the Theosophical Society's three declared objectives:

- To form a nucleus of the universal brotherhood of humanity, without distinction of race, creed, sex, caste, or color;
- To encourage the comparative study of religion, philosophy, and science;
- To investigate unexplained laws of nature and the powers latent in humanity.

Basic Terminology

People in specialized disciplines often use different terminology to describe the same object, and sometimes the same word to describe different energies. Following are definitions of some basic concepts that we will be working with—as taught to me by the Melchizedek lineage I am a part of, as they made these key concepts understandable to this ordinary human being who was struggling to master her new experiences of interdimensional awareness.

Who Are the Melchizedeks?

There are many different understandings of the term "Melchizedek." Some traditionalists feel it is the name of a Near Eastern priesthood whose beliefs are based on the teachings of the ancient priest named Melchizedek. Other traditions understand Melchizedek to be an aspect of Metatron, the consciousness said to sit at the right hand of God, who is the architect of many vast universes including our own. Some of these traditions feel Melchizedek took human incarnation to more fully understand humans and now serves from spirit.

Understandings about Melchizedek range from the beliefs of very strict conservative orders, which are patrilineal and only allow men to serve as priests, to the direct experiential mysticism of solitary practitioners ("solitaries") who have been contacted by, and receive instruction directly from, Metatron/Melchizedek himself. In the New Testament, Jesus is referred to as the High Priest of Melchizedek.[1]

The aspect of the Melchizedek energy that I work with consists of three coequals: Metatron, Melchizedek, and Michael. They have explained their distinctive qualities to me thus: Metatron is the architect/scientist, Melchizedek is the priest/teacher, and Michael is the warrior. This trio works with me, and many other solitaries, in an informal manner. "Call us the 3Ms," they say. They tell us jokes to lighten us up—humans can become very serious when first contacted by such an august team. I have met strangers in many parts of the country who work with the team as solitaries, and when we trade the jokes the 3Ms have told us, we recognize the similar consciousness.

The 3Ms insist—all of us solitaries are in agreement on this aspect of their teaching—that in an ultimate sense the 3Ms are not our guides but our colleagues, sitting with each of us at our own inner roundtable where we each have a responsibility and an equal say in what is to occur.

J. J. Hurtak, founder of the Academy for Future Science, describes the full range of Melchizedek practitioners as a scattered community of light—individual practitioners who have been a part of the order since their emergence from source, although they may not know this consciously. He states that the Melchizedek orders serve as coordinating points assisting heaven and earth to communicate with each other. The orders help maintain the correct order of the universes.

I learned about these energies when I was recovering from an environmental illness. They had been assisting me by letting me believe that my unusual insights as to how to heal myself were my own ideas—a common method of procedure for them. Eventually, Metatron identified himself and stated it was time I wake up and start helping out at a conscious level. The 3Ms had to first prove to me that they were real and not a figment of my imagination. After much testing of one another, we began working on a direct basis, and they have taught me everything of value that I now know.

The 3Ms explained that the universe is a vast place and the easiest way for me personally to learn is by direct experience. I was never to be leery about accepting an assignment or consultation because I couldn't understand at the outset how to solve an issue. If the 3Ms inwardly told me I should take the assignment, it became a new classroom for me. As promised, they have always provided the solution to the situation.

To learn more about the technical aspects of how the Melchizedeks work, read my second book *We Are Not Alone: A Complete Guide to Interdimensional Cooperation.* Also read Drunvalo Melchizedek's *The Ancient Secret of the Flower of Life* series, J. J. Hurtak's *The Book of Knowledge: The Keys of Enoch®*, and Alton Kamadon's Melchizedek Method publications. Each of these visionaries works directly with the Melchizedek energy in ways that are similar to what is being described here. However, each group focuses on a different aspect of evolving human consciousness. My area of specialization is helping people develop the ability to consciously cooperate with the many life forms who cohabit, or interact with, our Mother Earth.

What is a Merkabah?

In terms of spiritual science, the Melchizedeks teach that each drop of consciousness is its own world, each formed from the same one and only source. They call these drops and their combinations "merkabahs."

A merkabah is a ball of energy. It can be of any size; it can be part of another ball as well as host other balls. The universe itself is a huge merkabah.

A merkabah is formed when a single point of consciousness distances itself from its own energy to observe itself: to understand what it is and is not. This point of consciousness can fragment into any number of points as it self-explores to understand itself and to act. One depiction of the merkabah is the flower of life. (See Figure 0.1.)

The flower of life shows the field of the merkabah, which is formed of multiple subfields all co-existing.

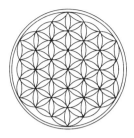

Figure 0.1. The flower of life.

The depiction of the polarity principles inherent in the merkabah is the star tetrahedron, known in the West as the Star of David and in the Far East as the center of the mandala of creation.

Figure 0.2. Star of David. Star tetrahedron. Mandala of creation.

At its simplest level, the star tetrahedron demonstrates the principles of polarity. The shape starts when a source energy splits to examine itself, creating a triangle. (In Figure 0.3, below, 1 = source, 2 = secondary split into polarities.) When each of the secondary energies split to respond to the question "Who am I?" by self-examining, a tertiary level develops on both sides, forming the star tetrahedron. (See Figure 0.4, below, numbering this 1—2—3 series of levels.)

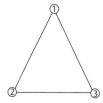 

Figure 0.3. Triangle.   Figure 0.4. Star tetrahedron.

In a well-functioning star tetrahedron, viewed in motion, the two triangles face each other, each spinning in the same direction—from the point of view of their common source point. But because they face, or oppose, each other, each triangle appears to the other triangle to be spinning in the opposite direction. As long as the two sides are balanced, this opposing motion self-sustains and self-clears each energy field. When one side seeks to dominate or control the other, imbalance occurs, which eventually causes a cascade of issues and a clogged interlocked energy field. This leads to conflict, as each side seeks to restore balance from its own perspective.[2]

A mature merkabah has many internal tracks uniting one aspect of the energy field with another. When the energy pauses to examine a specific location, a subsidiary merkabah is formed.

While motivations are universal, the methods of working with motivations and achieving goals will often vary significantly from one culture, world, or merkabah to another. There are many ways for a world to evolve, just as there are many ways for a human to personally evolve. These ways are dependent on environment, originating purpose, events that are individually encountered, and multiple experiences of events that become cultural to a particular society. This is true whether the life forms are amoeba, ants, specters, faeries, angels, orbs, intergalactic civilizations, or humans.

Our universe is, according to this vantage point, one merkabah whose energy keeps segmenting out to self-explore, establishing innumerable sub-merkabahs as it explores various aspects of its own energy. According to this viewpoint, there is nothing in the universe that is not of its overall parent form; even physical objects manufactured by humans contain the source and thus also have the potential for self-awareness.[3]

Adhering to this viewpoint permits an interdimensional communicator to return to source at any time in order to identify with an aspect of consciousness existing somewhere else inside the one all.

The 3Ms have shown me that the ability to communicate with any life form, at any location and time in space, reduces to the simple matter of identifying with that point's frequency, or stabilizing merkabah, and communicating with the life form in detachment and *ahimsa* (nonharm) via conscious oneness. Because all existence, even manufactured items, have at their source point emerged from the one, all existence is inherently conscious and capable of being communicated with. If all else fails, one can "simply" identify with source then, maintaining contact, descend from that point into the manifested form to establish communication. This does not mean you can solve the situation, but it does mean you can understand why the situation exists and what authentic options are available to you.

Working this way is, for me, an extension of the *bhakti* (devotional) yoga I have been practicing for thirty-odd years and of the Quaker tradition I was raised in, which focuses on the presence of divine light within each human being. I am an ordinary human being, and mine is a consciousness awareness, not a mental philosophical learning. For me, knowledge arises from the intelligence of the heart, which understands through identification with another, locating points of common ground. This common ground then forms a new, merged merkabah of understanding—a substance of existence that is felt and worked with. The mental functions, whose properties are to examine, separate, dissect, and explain, are purposely abandoned in the *bhakti* approach so that the eternally new situations that may be encountered can be entered into without prejudice. This is the art and science of the *bhakti* (*bhakti* practitioner), who separates to comprehend the multifarious other manifestations possible for the one beloved source, then merges to experience oneness with the beloved source who is cloaked in myriad forms.

So the philosophy inherent in this book comes from experiencing the reality of other forms of the one source, asking with awe "how is this possible?" and the source responding lovingly to show how and why. Using this approach, learning is via direct experience. The focus is not on mastering everything about a topic; first, because existence is vast in scope and it is impossible to learn everything; and second, because work is done in oneness with universal energy on a "need to know" basis—when new information is needed to work through a situation, you know you will have access to the right information at the right time in the right way.

ENERGY FIELDS

There are two primary ways in which to experience the organization of merkabah energy: as grids and as plasma. Grids are what occur as uncountable individual merkabahs join to create a stable field of energy, much like a woven window screen. Plasma is what occurs as merkabahs attach onto the screen and explore a specific function. These merkabahs join with others until the sheer bulk of their presence requires another stabilizing base. At this point, the plasma segments further, according to energy or interest, and becomes the base grid and plasma of the next energy segment. These interactions of plasma and grid form energy fields.

Merkabahs are like the base cells within a chameleon that can morph into whatever function is required: a tail, a leg, etc. Merkabahs exist in all sizes throughout the universe and morph as needed. Our third dimensional earth is a highly evolved merkabah that now provides a stable base for action in its particular frequency range.

People who sense the plasma are good at reading auras, the plasma field of life. People who see grids are gridworkers (such as myself) and are good at observing underlying structures.

DIMENSIONS

Every time a merkabah adapts for another function, it shifts its energy: its angle of spin, rate of spin, and speed of spin. As this function evolves, it eventually creates another dimension or world. This spinning functions as a merkabah, or contained globe of light/energy. Over time, this merkabah develops its own internal patterns of movement that can be tracked at the level of light and eventually can become so solid it obscures the light forms at its base. This occurs as the energy solidifies for concrete action inside its world. Gradually, over time, many sub-merkabahs form inside the parent. This is because the parent keeps segmenting to solve issues to form its own microworld.

Introduction

INTERDIMENSIONAL AND INTERWORLD COMMUNICATION AND
COOPERATION

As human consciousness expands, it becomes aware that it is not the only
conscious life form in this universe. Eventually, humans learn to communicate with these other life forms who exist close to our own frequency
(such as animals and plants) or further from our frequency (life forms in
other times, spaces of earth, or in other intergalactic worlds). These terms
are used almost interchangeably throughout this book: interdimensional
and interworld, and communication and cooperation. Communication implies understanding occurring, while cooperation implies action occurring
following the communication process.

People contain, and exist, in many dimensions and merkabahs simultaneously. But the density of the physical dimension prevents most people
from being aware of this. As people learn to see and sense energy, they
become aware of the wide variety of life forms both inside themselves and
surrounding themselves. Your body, for example, contains subworlds of
liver and spleen, and you can communicate with these parts of your body
as separate and aware consciousness beings, although few people in our
society ever do this.

When undertaking interdimensional communication, it is essential to
learn about boundaries, so that you can maintain your focus on whatever
issue you are working with, and can move into and out of various worlds
at will.

I believe many people diagnosed by Western science as insane are actually people who are experiencing other worlds but have not been taught
how to control this ability. Indigenous traditions keep an eye out for such
people and will take sensitive youth aside for training to be healers; our
culture tells them they are abnormal, so they attempt to stop their ability
to hear or see other life forms. And because they very often cannot, and
no one helps them understand what is happening, they set up one sad attempt after another to block this awareness. Sometimes these humans will
break down, unable to function, because they have become overwhelmed

by their unexplained experiences and their inability to stop this information from coming—remember, because it is interdimensional, it eludes third dimension walls.

The Melchizedeks explain that as our world is increasing in frequency capacity—part of the recurring cyclical shift of the ages—the walls between the dimensions are thinning. More and more humans are seeing or sensing images they cannot explain. The stories in this book show that these sightings are nothing more than the experiences in which humans connect with life in other dimensions. The stories show that interworld contact is normal, is nothing to be feared, and can benefit individuals and our world.

YOUR TEAM

I learned to sit with my team at an inner roundtable and put the topic of discussion in the middle; we work as a community, each with a say in a joint decision that will affect us all. Individual members of our team are knowledgeable in separate fields of consciousness and together, pooling our knowledge, we can achieve remarkable results. Most of you have forgotten this, and others have requested their teams to be quiet because they do not know what to make of these subtle energy contacts.

Your team usually includes at least one angel, as well as other life forms such as ascended masters; your ancestors; your soul family; your higher self; animal, rock, and plant totems; and perhaps the guiding spirit of the discipline in which you specialize (such as law, police work, art, music).

HIGHER SELF

People have many different levels of consciousness. The higher self is the individual's consciousness at a very high level of awareness—an illumined level that can assist its energetically denser level with advice and encouragement. Human beings eventually will evolve to a state in which they are a continuous conscious flow of energy from the higher self to the human level.

LEY LINES

The dowsing world calls the lines of energy that crisscross our earth "ley lines." The term originated with British dowsers who defined it as specific lines of energy that connected ancient religious sites to each other. It has evolved, as many words have, and now it is commonly used to refer to the various lines of energy that make up earth's stabilizing grids.

One of the most famous ley lines is the St. Michael line that connects major religious sites across England, lining up on a path followed by the sun on May 8—the spring festival of St. Michael. There are also lines of war that connect major battle sites and lines of power that connect major world capitals.

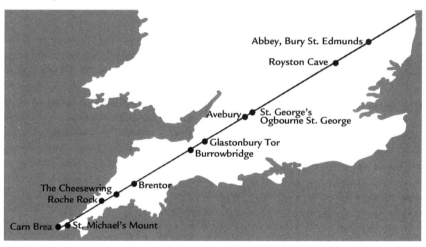

Figure 0.5. The St. Michael line, as it crosses England, with the major religious sites along its route.

Ley lines exist at all levels and frequencies; they are part of the grid energies, or light fields, that underlie all existence. The presence of benevolently energized, infected, or discordant ley lines on a property can profoundly affect the energy of the people, plants, animals, and other life forms in that area, for better or worse. They are one of the first things a land dowser looks for. Ley lines can be dowsed, felt, and observed (a line of trees all leaning in one direction, or a line where no plants are growing).

Major ley lines such as the St. Michael line are so deep and so interconnected to the earth and the millions of subsidiary energies along the line that it is very difficult, if you want to work along the path of that line, to adapt the energy to anything other than what it is currently transmitting. This is especially true if the location is a nodal point on the line (a location held in place by the crossing of ley lines). It is best in this situation to explore why an individual or a company chose subconsciously to locate along that line. A ley line with few stabilizing nodes can often be altered to meet local needs, which is a craft many dowsers practice.

VORTEXES AND PORTALS

When two lines of energy cross, their energies affect each other. The crossing can cause a spin, or vortex. When multiple lines cross, the vortex is stronger.

This is one way a portal exists. A portal is a gateway to another world. Portals are one of the issues an interdimensional communicator works with, for many accidents or occurrences can affect their proper working. You'll find a number of stories about portals in this book.

KALI YUGA

Hinduism, Buddhism, yoga, and other traditions consider time to be cyclical in nature, a spiral moving forward in a circular motion. There is a very long cycle called the cycle of ages, which different Hindu traditions variously identify as several thousand years to 26,000 years or more.

The lowest level of consciousness in the cycle of ages is the Kali Yuga, the Age of Darkness, when the capacity to see into other dimensions is the dullest. Many great yogis, such as Sri Aurobindo, believe we have now completed this age. The end of the Kali Yuga heralds the dawning of the Satya Yuga—the Golden Age of Spirituality—the start of the next cycle when consciousness is at its highest. Many people believe that we are currently experiencing this shift; humanity is waking up to self-awareness.

The dates of this shift and whether it will occur peacefully or catastrophically vary according to the beliefs of different traditions. There is also division over whether our world wars and our current upheavals mark the end of the Kali Yuga or the birth pangs of the Golden Age.

Be this as it may, segments of many world traditions, as well as many futurists and soothsayers, are presenting us with a common theme for our time: the end of one world consciousness and the start of another. Remarkably similar time frames are posited by proponents of the Hindu Kali Yuga, the Christian Second Coming of Christ, the Navajo end of the fourth world, Nostradamus's end of time, and the Mayan end of calendar (various Mayan groups specify dates somewhere between 2001 and 2042). It is my personal belief, as explained to me by the 3Ms, that our current world unrest is the result of the forces dominant during the Kali Yuga being replaced by the more aware forces of the dawning Age of Spirituality.

ORBS, PLASMA, AND SPIRIT IMAGES

Orbs—round balls of light—are the plasma of some life forms who are visible to human eyes or to cameras. Right now, no one knows for sure exactly what we are seeing when we look at orbs. It is my personal experience that we are looking at life forms whose frequency is different from ours and that we are seeing many different life forms. We can identify with the life form frequency sufficiently to see its life force energy (aura), which is formed at a more common level of higher consciousness, but below that— e.g., at frequencies that approach those of matter—our shapes diverge sufficiently so that we can no longer see the form.

Many orbs are nature spirits who enjoy being around happy energy; they are often seen at parties and spiritual gatherings. Some people see the nature spirit as an orb, others see the same spirit in its subtle physical form as a faery with arms and legs, etc. There are many drawings of faeries, depicted by the same clairvoyants, as variously orbs, human forms, and a human form emerging from a globe of light.

Some orbs may be seen in the shape of spirits of departed loved ones or as cosmic energies, and some may be biological vehicles that are used by various intergalactic worlds to travel through time/space. I have watched orbs appear and then transform into plasma "mist," and I have seen many orb photos in which geometric shapes, faces, and whole bodies are apparent.

Orbs are conscious life forms who are aware of their human colleagues and can come to a location when called by an aware human being or when their energetic assistance is required. Cameras, especially digital cameras, are quite able to record their presence when an aware photographer consciously requests it.

Figure 0.6 is a photograph of multiple orbs, as well as several orbs combining into a branch or grid, taken by Melanie J. France, a colleague who is guardian of the Bluff Trail Labyrinth in Wisconsin.

Figure 0.6. Orbs attracted to a very flat labyrinth. There is no plant growing in the middle—that is a branch formed of orbs!

Figure 0.7 is a photograph taken by Lanette Padula at one of my nature spirit photography workshops; it was taken at dusk and clearly shows a plasma bear, her totem, appearing in a field behind an energy-rich prairie and in front of pine trees.

Figure 0.7. Bear totem.

Different people perceive energy in different ways, and this translates into what their cameras, who have synchronized with the owner's energy, will capture. (The findings of quantum physics are applicable here: the intent of the observer—the photographer—affects the field being observed.)

I have been working to see the energies manifest in the physical world and my images are very solid. Figure 0.8 is an image of a spirit bear—my totem animal—appearing as a burr[4] on a burr oak tree.

Figure 0.8. Burr oak bear totem.

NATURE SPIRITS

This is a common term used to describe life forms who are involved with the care of earth's plants, trees, rocks, air, animals, etc. They have been termed "spirits" because they exist in a less solid world than our own and, to most humans, appear not to have solid form. In their own world, which exists in a different dimension or frequency than ours, these life forms do have substance, but it is not the solid form of our world—a situation that has its benefits and drawbacks. The benefit is that form is far more supple for nature spirits and they can affect the life force energy, changing to a certain extent their own appearance and the life force energy of plants. The drawback is that if a problem is grounded in a physical situation, such as a human-polluted river affecting the life force of their charges, they are unable to change the situation by themselves. They need the cooperation of a human to make the physical change. This need for human assistance is the real reason humans are called the stewards of earth. Humans are responsible for understanding, arbitrating, and manifesting on the physical plane of earth the will and wishes of other often-competing dimensions.

Energetically, nature spirit/human interaction on a piece of land is similar to a human deciding whether to go to a holistic practitioner or a surgeon for a health situation: each realm has its strong points and weaknesses and ultimately needs to cooperate with the efforts of practitioners from other realms to complete a complex task.

In recent times, nature spirits and ordinary humans did not mix a great deal. Nature spirits did not trust humans, who have more complex vital energies that can keep the humans locked in the realm of powerful, sometimes violent, emotions.

Nowadays, however, many energy workers are experiencing the return of the nature beings' interaction with humans. This is occurring for several reasons. One is that our own human consciousness is evolving to the point where many people can peacefully relate with nature.

Another reason is that earth is at a very critical juncture in its evolution. We now have the opportunity to destroy ourselves and very seriously damage our earth. If we destroy our earth, we destroy the nature beings' home as well. It is therefore very strongly in the interest of the nature spirits to cooperate with, and assist, those humans who are willing to help our common earth home transform into something better.

If we are fortunate enough to be in contact with nature spirits and earth energies, we have a certain obligation. With no one to teach me, I had to learn operating procedures through sometimes sad experiences. I hope the stories and lessons in this book provide you with ways to communicate with nature spirits, as well as things to avoid doing.

A technical note: There are many definitions of the terms I use to discuss nature spirits. When we humans attempt to translate consciousness-communicated terms into solid third-dimension words, there is necessarily a certain amount of semantic confusion. The definitions I've used are a result of how I have translated the information provided me by the consciousness of the nature spirit realm as we worked on a commonality of understanding to pursue some cooperative action. Nature spirits often explain to a human that they are "like" something the human is familiar with, so our personal experiences affect our understanding of the life forms we encounter.

"Nature spirits" refers to the entire range of life forms who work within the nature realm. "Faery" refers to some of the life forms who work in the nature realms, such as fairies, devas, elves, gnomes, and trolls. "Fairy" refers to a specific species within the faery realm who operates at a worker level caring for specific plants, trees, and stones; they are sometimes mischievous.

The supervisor level of the fairies are the "nature devas." Nature devas, or simply devas, are more serious in their work and have an internal hierarchy ranging from devas in charge of the fairies of a specific area to devas in charge of other devas and on up to an overall Earth Deva herself. The devas make certain all works well in their assigned area of earth; they are often very innovative in their solutions to problems of their area and are very task oriented. They can mete out punishments to irresponsible fairies and can be punished themselves for failure to protect and enrich their area of responsibility.

Ghosts, Break Offs, Spirits of Place, and Thought Forms

Some people call anything they cannot define that is moving through a space a ghost. In actuality, the life form in any particular space could have its origin in many different worlds, ranging from nature spirits to extraterrestrials.

A "ghost" is the subtle energetic existence of a once-solid human being or animal who has "died" but has not yet left the earth plane. A ghost exists in a blue-grey realm of energy and is locked to the earth plane until some issue has been resolved: a task is completed, a message is given to someone, or the ghost is simply provided the knowledge that he or she is dead and can go to the light. A ghost can be communicated with and can respond.

Often mistaken for a ghost is a "break off." This is part of the energy field of a person or animal that broke off during an incident of intense emotion, such as a violent death. A break off has more color than a ghost because it retains the color of the particular moment in which it was formed. It keeps repeating the same motion and you cannot communicate with it. It is not aware of you; it is like a video that keeps replaying.

Some energy forms often mistaken for ghosts are "guardians of place" and "spirits of place." These are conscious life forms who can be in charge of places—from a small spring to a vast region, such as a national park. These spirits are generally benign, unless you are out to damage their domain. A spirit of place is usually a nature spirit or angel. Guardians of place have sometimes been humans who have chosen to remain on a piece of property as a protector.

Guardians of place can also be thought forms. Humans often create thought forms—such as a lack of self-worth or an obsession with a particular activity—unconsciously, and they grow to control us. These thought forms can take on a life as solid for us as our building a physical home.

But, in general, "thought form" refers to a being consciously materialized by an occultist to protect something. The Native American medicine people sometimes created these to protect a place such as a spring essential to their tribe's survival. The thought form is created and given a specific task. While most thought forms are somewhat primitive when formed, once created, they start to evolve. They have a crafty intelligence because they have to adapt to defend their charges. Over time, the accumulation of thought forms' experiences cause them to morph in form. They almost always retain the thought that formed them as their guiding principle. This can make them difficult and dangerous to work with—for instance, when an unconscious builder places a home on the site that a thought form was created to protect.

Annie Besant and C. W. Leadbeater of the Theosophical Society wrote the book *Thought Forms* in which they explored the nature and power of thoughts. They divided thought forms into three classes: (1) those that take the image of the thinker; (2) those that take the image of some material object; and (3) those that take forms entirely their own, expressing their inherent qualities in the matter that they draw around them.

A Treatise on Cosmic Fire by Alice Bailey and Djwhal Khul, published by the Lucis Trust, also touches on thought forms and how to work with them. Alice Bailey describes an experiment to see if she could manifest a thought form into existence. She did eventually achieve this, only to discover it was not controllable by her and that it caused problems for other people. She then had to dematerialize it—a difficult task—and subsequently stopped experimenting in that area. This was an experiment done from a Western cultural perspective.

Medicine people in indigenous cultures and Eastern occultists have long traditions for manifesting and working with thought forms. The bottom line in all traditions is that thought forms can be mavericks, can morph out of control, and are one of the trickier energies to work with.

Introduction

How Interworld Cooperation Works

"Interworld cooperation," "interdimensional cooperation": these are terms acknowledging that this universe contains many different worlds filled with conscious life forms. These worlds exist at different frequencies. Above local time and space, different worlds can coexist in the same space without interfering with one another. Each form operates within a different frequency, rate and degree of spin, within the infinite options of the one whole. Situations occur in which two parallel dimensions bleed into each other and people see or sense other life forms cohabiting their space. That's often when I am called in for help!

The mechanics of this are covered in my previous book, *We Are Not Alone: A Complete Guide to Interdimensional Cooperation.*

Currently, we are entering into a new world where consciousness is expanding and refining. It is part of the natural cycle of time: a new Golden Age is approaching in which people are aware of subtle energy. During this phase, the veils between dimensions are thinning, and we are able to see into them far more easily than ever before.

Our evolving technology is assisting with this; new digital imaging devices are capturing subtle frequencies often unseen by the human eye.

Each of us has an affinity for various other worlds because of our inherent energy make-up. If a gnome and a unicorn appear in an area, some people in a group will see one and some the other. This affinity explains why several people photographing the same scene will get different subtle energy forms in their images.

An experienced communicator is able to travel through frequencies to locate the world/dimension in which an issue exists for a specific situation or client. Such a communicator can move through time—backward, forward, and sideways—as well as through spatial differentials of frequency, rate of spin, and degree of rotation. Put another way, wherever the issue originated and is causing a problem, interdimensional communicators can locate it, *if*: (1) they can acknowledge that such a place and life form is possible, or they are willing to believe that their inner team is able to see and work with diverse worlds that humans are not aware of; (2) they have sufficiently cleaned up their own personal act so that the issue is one they are willing to work with; and (3) they have learned detachment, the ability to adjust quickly, and to work in cooperation with their reliable inner team from various dimensions.

The universe has the energies of both the mother and the father. It has a way of protecting its own children. We only receive the lessons we are capable of handling; the other lessons remain hidden until it is time for us to grow into greater knowledge. When you are eager to learn and you can maintain a responsible attitude, you will be presented with many opportunities to expand. However, if you are unable to acknowledge that such opportunities exist, even if a fairy or an angel stands right in front of you, your consciousness will refuse to acknowledge its presence and you will swear there is nothing there—despite the fact that people around you see it and tell you what the life form looks like! This has happened on occasion in my workshops, and it is sadly amusing.

EXERCISES

Experience is always the best instructor. Therefore you have the opportunity to experience the principles being discussed via exercises. The exercises are simple, to the point, and safe. However, when working with energy, nothing is ever one hundred percent guaranteed, so for your own protection it is wise to invoke whatever forces of light, love, and protection you generally work with. If you do not yet consciously work with inner colleagues, now is the time to start doing so!

You can always powerfully invoke the protection of Archangel Michael. This archangel is the energy in charge of preparing and moving humanity into the next era of earth's development. His is a vast consciousness with many aspects and assistants, and he can easily be many places at once!

To protect yourself, you can invoke the high beings of whatever tradition you happen to practice—such as Christ, Buddha, Mary, or White Buffalo Calf Woman.

Should you be more abstractly oriented, you can place before you the image of a powerful piece of sacred geometry such as a merkabah, a flower of life, or a cross; these images help you to center and work from safe space.

Or if you are sound-oriented you can chant to invoke peace and love—nothing dark can exist inside these high-frequency fields of consciousness.

Then go slowly and carefully. If something does not feel right to you, call a stop to the exercise until you have a chance to assess it. The forces of light are patient and understand your need to check your facts. The dark forces are the ones who want you to hurry up and act—before you have a chance to check things out; dark forces may tell you that they are safe, trust them; or they may act insulted that you would question them. There are shills and rogues in all dimensions!

When you start an exercise, ask the energies you are working with to provide you with an effective test that will demonstrate their ability to assist you. Then check whether they actually complete the task as they have promised. Examine yourself, and see where you have unwarranted prejudices that you can work to overcome.

Before you do each exercise in the book, remember to set the stage and invoke protection.

I still follow this procedure—invoking protection and setting up a merkabah for the situation with which I'm working. In energy work, this is called "setting space" and then "holding space." "Setting space" refers to the process by which grid workers set the stage to safely perform their work. In my case, I inwardly invoke my team—the 3Ms and whatever guides are involved in this situation—for my personal protection. I then request the light guides of the client and the situation to be present.

Next I invoke a stream of light descending from God the Father (vision or unmanifest consciousness) and anchored in God the Mother (matter or fully manifested consciousness)—two polarities of the one ultimate unity. Along the line of this stream is the frequency of the issue to be worked with. I energetically locate and focus on this point—the "soul" of the issue. I see the point expand into a merkabah—a globe of light. I request permission of the light source soul energies of the situation to allow me to work with them for an appropriate solution. If permission is not granted, I work with the energies to solve that first necessity. Usually it means clients have presented their side of the story and the energy being worked with doesn't agree—they see the matter differently. So I listen to their perception of the matter. When they understand I have come to be of assistance and permission is granted, I begin work.

In other words, I make sure clients, their guides, and the guides of the situation can consciously communicate with one another. I create a safe space for all the parties involved, a place where all the different frequencies can come together in a safe environment and consciously discuss the issues of common concern.

Another way to express this: I connect frequencies so that the various parties to a situation are communicating on a common wave length and thus are mutually intelligible to one another. Then we can discuss, negotiate, argue, and make peace as we work toward a mutually acceptable conclusion.

At the end of the session, the client and I close the space. Inwardly, I always offer gratitude to my team and to all the energies involved—this is very important as cosmic energies should always be respected and appreciated, for what they give they can also take away if they deem us rude or ungrateful and thus unworthy of their assistance.

Photographs

Photographing spirits is becoming increasingly common and interesting, with the increasing sophistication of digital cameras, better processing using Photoshop and other computer programs, and the thinning of the veils between dimensions that is occurring.

Many people are capturing interdimensional life forms. Many do so unconsciously, thinking their camera is defective when they view images of orbs, plasma, and spirits who have manifested as round balls, plasma, and mist in their photos. Many other people photograph life forms consciously and, in a group taking photos of the same location, different types of spirits will be seen in the photographs taken by different people.

We have a local group called the Blue Papaya—members are advanced perception youths. The group is sponsored by ISIC (the Institute for the Study of Interdimensional Cooperation) and Crystal Life Technology. (You can visit Blue Papaya on Facebook.) During the summer, the youths visit local nature preserves to learn how to communicate with and photograph life forms of other worlds. Parents usually accompany their youth and they too take photographs. This is a wonderful learning experience for all. We learned that within the group, some people have an affinity for trees, others for faeries, still others for animal spirits. Photographing the same area, one child will get images of his favored life forms while a child next to him records something totally different.

Some children, however, are deterred from capturing images by their Western cultural and/or religious drilling that any type of experience not of the solid third dimension is inherently evil and to be avoided. These constricted children learn from the longer-time members and soon open up, thrilled to find a way that validates their experience that other life forms are present and they can communicate with them. When children can say, "There is a life form over by that fir tree," and then take a photo of that location and have an orb or plasma appear, it is a solid validation of their ability. It greatly soothes the children's parents as well, for many have been told by school counselors that their children need counseling and drugs to correct their wild imaginations!

Unfortunately, most of the parents say their biggest issue with their advanced perception children is teaching them the necessity of not saying anything to others about what they can see and hear. The sad reality is that, currently, sharing their perceptions labels these children "weird" and hurts their ability to interact with "ordinary" schoolmates.

As mentioned earlier, everything in the universe is alive and conscious—including manufactured objects, which are made of consciousness and are affected by their surroundings, evolving in accordance with their experiences. A chair sat on by a holy man will eventually have a different energy from a chair that is repeatedly sat on by a man who beats his wife and children. In some basic way, people understand this, and most would prefer to own the holy man's chair because of its association and the feeling of the holiness it embodies.

In a similar way, a camera is affected by the person who works with it. This is an experiential reality. Many energy worker photographers have discovered that as they work to capture a certain reality, it becomes easier for their camera to record it—plasma, orb, or spirit form. If they hand their cameras to other people, very often such people will, for an hour or so, be able to capture these images as well. But then their less-aware consciousness begins to pervade the camera, and the ability of the camera to record subtle energy begins to fade.

People have been able to record spirit with all types of cameras. There are some commonalities to current camera technology. With the advent of digital cameras, the appearance of spirit forms has increased. The digital cameras are somewhat similar to computers, capturing information in code and transferring that into images. The simpler point-and-shoot digital cameras often do not have infrared correction in them. Many of the orb life forms inhabit the infrared frequencies and thus are picked up quite well with these cameras. Unfortunately, these cameras usually do not have a high pixel density, and this means the orbs cannot be blown up to any great degree to get good detail.

I have found that many of the higher-end digital cameras (such as my Nikon D80) with greater pixel depth are also able to record orbs, but the orbs they record seem to be those who live in a different and higher frequency than the infrared orbs. It is even more difficult to record spirit orbs with the newer crystalline technology that debuted with the Nikon D90. On the other hand, my Nikon D90 takes the best photos to date of nature spirits who manifest in trees, rocks, plants, and land; it can record the fine detail of these spirits, who exist in a subtle form that can be seen with the human eye but often slips out of range with a camera. I usually work with my D90, because I enjoy my interactions with the nature spirits of trees and rocks.

Our Blue Papaya group has produced wonderful results shooting with cell phone cameras and point-and-shoot cameras, printing their photos at the nearest photo lab. Other people use a simple computer photo program to print. For those who share my more technical interest, to clearly record nature spirits, here is my process: I shoot in Camera Raw, using a Nikon D90; process via Lightroom and Photoshop; and print on an Epson ink jet printer. This system allows the most pliable use of contrast to bring forward details that tend to get lost with the older cameras.

Throughout this book, you will find tips on how to best photograph various types of life forms, using common current technology. However, technology is evolving rapidly, and I am certain some expert eventually will begin adapting cameras for more accurate depiction of other frequencies.

Wherever you are in your knowledge of photography, just get out and shoot! Don't delete anything unless it is really, really bad! I have gone back to my old photographs, taken years before, and found some wonderful new information.

When I started, I knew nothing about photography and was only shooting because my inner colleagues requested I do so. The topic intrigued me, once I saw the life forms, but it also distressed me that my skills were not equal to the information being provided by the nature realm. So I began taking classes in photography and in Photoshop, and at the same time this technology was also rapidly advancing. Now I have advanced to being able to bring the subtle energies to the fore in the same images in which I once just saw "something." For your interest, note Figures 4.9 through 4.12: these were my very first photos of nature spirits, and, honestly, I'd only taken maybe two hundred photos before in my whole life! So their quality is not as good as the situation warranted.

I shoot in color. In preparation for this book, I converted these photos to black and white and learned that doing so reveals underlying forms inherent in the scene. The series of the Indian village shows this situation, especially the recording of the thought forms the medicine man wove into his circle. In Figure 2.4 of the medicine man's seat, it was now apparent that the medicine man's energy had embedded itself inside the end of the seat. See his profile. In Figure 2.8, which I included to show *one* thought form discernible in color, I discovered two or three were revealed in the black and white image! In the story of the bog orb (Figure 3.8), you can see greater detail. The profile of the bog orb's face, which is in front of the tree to the left, is now visible, and he is looking toward a spirit dolphin on the far side of that tree, which makes sense, given that he is from the water world—he's showing that he wants to return there! Colleagues looking at the image pointed out many other images there as well; this hillock has a lot of spirit energy moving about it!

I encourage you not to throw out that photograph with the "specks of dust" ruining the image, or the one with the bright white stripe, or the three multiples you took of the same scene. What appears at first to be a glitch may upon closer examination yield something more interesting, and orbs and spirits will often appear in one scene and not another, for they move about just like we do.

If this craft of photographing beings of other realms appeals to you, invest in a good camera and some lessons in Photoshop!

• 1 •

Ghosts and Spirits

A Visit from the Angel of Death

Nana had died a few days ago. She'd had a tough life, her husband dying at a young age, leaving her with young boys to rear at a time when it was not respectable in some circles for women to work outside the home. But she had done so. In her old age, she became cantankerous, domineering, and demanding, eventually dying in a nursing home because none of her children wanted to have her stay with them.

As the only girl grandchild, I had been a favorite of Nana's, and that evening, as my husband and I were peacefully reading, I felt a sudden swoop of energy into the room. Just as suddenly I felt compelled to speak out. "It's a shame no one will miss my grandmother," I said to my husband. "She was such a crotchety old woman, no one liked to be around her." He looked up, nodded, and returned to reading.

But as these words hit the air, the room filled with a profound, grey sadness; it was clear Nana's spirit was present and had heard. I felt a rush of guilt for saying something so unkind, but an angelic presence whispered to me that he had compelled me to speak the truth, and from that uttered truth a new level of communication between Nana and the angel was now occurring. There was a sudden shift of energy as Nana accepted that the way she had been treated by her relatives had been directly caused by her own behavior. That permitted her to let go of her weighty anchor of bitterness. Peace descended. Then there was a swoosh of angel wings as the Angel of Death and the now-at-peace Nana continued their journey, unimpeded, to the other side.

LESSONS

Very often the Angel of Death will help people to understand their life better by bringing them to where loved ones are and surrounding the situation with a truth light. The light causes the loved ones to state their real feelings about the person who just crossed over. There are many reasons for this. Sometimes it is to help spirits move through a state of illusion in which they feel unjustly treated—to reveal the reality of the situation. In other cases, it is to reassure the living that life is indeed eternal and their loved ones still exist, just not in the same way as before.

EXERCISE

People experience death in so many ways—described by so many books. In my work, I have seen a variety of scenarios, including lost and bewildered spirits hanging out at the site where they died and in "picnic groves" where the dead congregate, angry spirits seeking revenge and spirits who are being held in the earth plane by their attachment to another person or a place. I have not seen any ghosts of people who were loved and whose loved ones prayed for them to transition to the light/God/Jesus/Buddha/source—however source is perceived. The love of those close to the transitioning person—whether of this world or of their team in other worlds—surrounds spirits and helps them move on into the next room that spirit is meant to inhabit.

If, from false understanding, loved ones attempt to hold the departed in contact, they can actually prevent spirits from transitioning to the light. In this case spirits exist in a blue-grey intermediate zone, a place that is not particularly happy and where the spirits do not get fed the food of light. It is always better to pray for the departed to safely transition to the light. Once they have passed through those gates, they will return as light, if they wish to and if the situation warrants it. As light, they can be of significant help to their loved ones still on earth, protecting, inspiring, and offering wisdom that now is more profound than ever for it is coming from pure spirit.

Once souls have transitioned to the light, their human shortcomings are left behind, and they exist once again as pure souls who had high aspirations to do well on earth. Having experienced human form, they are especially able to appreciate the problems of earth and can work to significantly alleviate these problems for their loved ones. Before loved ones transition, their human frailties are still very much present and issues such as jealousy, control, and possessiveness can be present in their interactions with their loved ones. When they have fully crossed over, good but imperfect humans leave these issues behind, and they come back to visit or assist as pure soul-light.

Sit quietly, center yourself. Then look back over your own life and those of loved ones who have passed over. Say a prayer of positive intent for them, requesting that they be fully and happily transitioned to the light (they may have long ago transitioned, but just in case . . .). If you discover loved ones are still on the earth plane and have not transitioned to the light, seek the reason and help them to complete unfinished business so that they can leave, or help them work through an alternate solution to their unfinished business. If they have transitioned, focus on the loved ones and the happy times of the past. Send them love, and request that they bless you with their own love. If you need help, tell them what it is and ask if they can assist you.

PHOTOGRAPHS

My company, Crystal Life Technology, has an annual spirit photography contest at its store. One year we received photographic submissions from a mother whose two grown children had died within a few months of each other. Each of her children had young children of their own. She sent us photographs of the uniquely identifiable energy orbs that she at first unexpectedly captured on camera and in subsequent gatherings looked to photograph. At each holiday gathering, a specific unique orb was seen next to each of her grandchildren. The grandmother believes these are the spirits of each child's dead parent, coming to be present with their children at the family gatherings. In this woman's case, we concluded she was able to capture the shapes of the spirit orbs because her children had transitioned and then returned as complete energy forms.

Very often, when people are just starting to understand interdimensional life energy, they think it is fun to go to known haunted sites and take photographs of the spirits. While this is indeed "fun," there are serious considerations involved: What are you capable of doing in such a situation? Can you protect yourself if this is needed? Do you have the capacity to deal with any ramifications, or do you need to go in the company of a true energy expert? Are you observing a ghost, guardian of place, or perhaps even a hostile entity who might cause problems?

To date, photographing ghost manifestation has not been an area I have chosen to focus on. However, there are many photographs on the Internet and in esoteric books of ghosts and spirits. My interest in approaching ghosts is for the purpose of correcting a situation. With clients, I first ascertain that they really want the situation to be corrected. If they are just curious and want to confirm their feeling but don't want the ghost transitioned, I do not accept the consultation. If they want help, I am focused on providing that; I seek to immediately connect with the ghost and, through the surprise of that, negotiate more easily for a successful transition. Recording photographically would entail detaching, calling the ghost in, photographing it—and by that time, the ghost has settled into the ways that have prevented transition, hence making it very difficult to achieve.

MANY DOORS LEAD TO THE BEYOND

Fran and Jim work with energetic sound technology and exhibit at various shows around the country. When our shows coincide, we go out for dinner and catch up. Many years ago, when I was new to this work, we went out for a Chinese meal.

As we settled in at the restaurant booth, Fran was clearly distracted. Finally she said to the air, "I know, I know, you want to go with the angels. We told you, your cousin Edith is waiting to take you to the other side. Please go with her."

"It's my mother, Marion," Jim explained. "She transitioned several months ago but is stuck just on this side of the opening. We've been arguing the point for weeks. She won't go with Edith; she wants to go with the angels!"

He sighed in exasperation. "Mom was always bossy in this life, and she's still doing it in the other! It's upsetting my wife. Mom won't stop nagging her about it. We've gotten as far as determining Mom is looking for a special door to go through," he said. "And that it is on a parallel plane to the one we keep showing her. Mom doesn't want to go the way we are showing."

As he spoke, he unconsciously drew his hand along a horizontal line in front of him, describing the situation.

I was casually looking at what he was doing and something about the sweep didn't feel quite right. "Oh," I said, "You mean she wants to go here." I drew my hand along a horizontal line, making an energetic correction in how he was moving.

This changed direction created a sudden eagerness in the air. Fran, Jim, and I all felt it, and looked at each other in surprise.

The mother's spirit was very excited. "Do it again," the mother spirit prodded me.

I obliged, repeating the sweeping movement. This time, when that same point was reached, it became clear what was occurring, and I moved my hand upward, following the energy. "The angelic door she's looking for is here."

The three of us felt a rush of energy as the spirit of the mother eagerly flew through the newly located door. The force of her exit physically pulled us up with a soft jump.

We three humans looked at each other in surprise, vividly aware that Marion's intense presence was no longer with us.

That night, when I was asleep, the mother returned to thank me. She had crossed over into the light and was exactly where she knew she should be. She requested a favor. "Please," she said, "Tell my son and his wife this. When you go into the other world, beyond death, there are many rooms to enter. You don't have to choose one you don't want, and there is not just one route. Tell them to offer a choice of doors to those they are helping."

Lessons

Dead people are supposed to cross over into the light seamlessly. If they don't, what went wrong? Doors (portals) are supposed to open to let the dead pass through; if they don't open or the dead don't pass through, what has occurred and why?

The universe is a huge light grid—like the earth seen at night from the sky, with its multiple points of electric lights. The wiring of this universal light field descends in frequency from source to solid form, source being the main power plant feeding out to successive layers of subsidiary stations, all the way down to our own bodies.

In my work with energy, I function like an electrician—checking lines, adjusting circuits as needed, putting in new transformers, and rewiring lines to properly connect and avoid overloading.

Each situation has its own problems inherent to its field. Thus, the questions to be addressed are: *What is happening to the field in the area we are observing? Where has the wiring gone wrong?* Proper functioning is the desired state; faulty functioning needs to be corrected.

EXERCISE

Practice looking into the light, seeing what is at the end of the tunnel. Or sit in a room and pretend you are looking at doors that lead to the beyond. What do you think lies behind each door? What are your options? What, then, are your options for how you are going to live your life now, so that when you die you can easily go through the door you wish to experience.

THE GHOST WHO WASHED DISHES

Three energy workers—Jody, Cynthia, and I—gathered in Kevin and Corey MacFarland's family room to listen to their story. The couple was opening a meditation center in northern Illinois. They were especially sensitive to subtle energies and complained about "things" moving through rooms and through their property—things they could not identify—and they wanted energetic assistance.

This is a wonderful aspect of working with energy practitioners. We are aware that consciousness is infinite, and while we may have mastered some aspects of it, there is much yet to know. Therefore, when there is a situation we cannot work out, we will seek out practitioners who may have chosen to specialize in that area. We then will learn from them and incorporate the new knowledge into our own practice!

This was some years ago, near the start of my practice, and our little practitioner group was experimenting with what could be seen in the same area when different energy workers observed it, using different modalities. Jody and I would be leading workshops at the couple's center, and Cynthia was a budding energy worker in training. We decided to split up, look around, then come back together and see what the different overall results were. Jody and Cynthia went upstairs—a newer part of the house where the owners were having some issues, and I focused on the first floor and basement—part of which was the original historic prairie farmhouse.

Practitioners can turn interdimensional perception on and off at will—otherwise they would go into overload from so many different voices and life forms occupying the same space. I turned on my internal scanning mode, adjusting it to perceive the issues the family wanted assistance with, and started looking around. I left Kevin and Corey in the living room and walked into the kitchen, which was part of the original farmhouse. In a sudden energy shift, where there was now a third-dimension stove and stove hood, a prairie woman in a faded plaid dress was washing dishes at a phantom sink and stacking them above her in a phantom cupboard. This was becoming interesting!

Moving on, I entered the dining room where I saw a group of very frightened nature spirits huddled in the corner like disheveled refugees.

The living room and foyer were very peaceful; this is where the couple currently held their meditation sessions, and meditative energy had washed the rooms clean.

Then it was down to the basement where more of the nature spirits were pathetically positioned near a sealed portal that had once been the gateway between their world and ours. The portal had been in the stonework above the fireplace, which had deteriorated to such an extent that Kevin had recently redone and recemented the wall. Alas, this had also destroyed the gateway to the nature spirits' world. The original deterioration had been due in part to all the activity through that area!

These nature spirits reminded me of someone . . . and I suddenly realized it was Kevin; he even had the same slightly pointed ears as these beings! Kevin had an energetic tie to these faeries. It appeared he had unconsciously been attracted to the property because of its "familiar" energy; but because he did not know about subtle land energies, he had no awareness of the deep reasons for the distressed energies he and his wife could sense.

I returned to the living room and, while waiting for my two colleagues to return, chatted with the couple. "How old is this section of the house?" I asked them, pointing to their modern-looking kitchen.

The woman looked surprised. "It dates back to the original structure, which we think was from the 1800s," she said.

"Are you aware of anything moving around in the kitchen?" I asked.

Corey hesitated and looked at her husband, seeking his agreement for her to continue. He nodded.

"Yes . . . we are," Corey said slowly.

I described the spirit, and the couple nodded. "We have seen her for some time now, dressed exactly like that," Corey said. "And she is beginning to materialize more strongly."

My two colleagues returned then from their trip upstairs, and the five of us discussed the energies of the house.

It was decided that for the short time remaining before we had to go to other appointments, we would work on the most immediate concerns; we would return later to work on the other issues.

The first task was to work with the upstairs ley lines that were affecting the family's sleep. We cleared several vortexes and worked to clear a ley line that passed through the couple's bedroom. However, this ley line was anchored outside the dwelling in some small stands of trees that were growing on either side of the house. For the time being, we could only temporarily clear the bedroom. The source needed to be cleared as well. We placed some meditation statues on either side of the ley line as it passed through the room and recommended the couple focus on the statues from time to time to keep their protective energies active.

We then moved to the basement and opened the portal so the frightened nature beings could go back home. We suggested Kevin might enjoy sitting by the portal from time to time, to converse with the faeries. They considered him their protector in this world, and their energy would help elevate and lighten his own, when work issues troubled him.

This was all we had time to work with on this visit.

Several weeks later our trio gathered again at the couple's retreat center/home. We arrived while the couple was away on a business call, so we walked about outside. The first site of interest was a stand of trees in the front of the property where one side of the bedroom ley line was anchored. As we entered the woods, we saw many different groups of spirits gathered there. It was a picnic grove for spirits! To the right were some Civil War–era soldiers eating chow around a fire; other spirits were peeking out at us from behind trees. Coming toward us, from the house, was the prairie woman in the faded plaid dress.

Once again our small group split up our tasks. Jody and Cynthia focused on the spirits in the clearing, sending the various groups to the light so that they could continue their soul evolution. I focused on the woman with the dishes.

The woman was very worried; the burden of responsibility weighed heavily on her. Her peaceful little prairie home, with the chickens running about outside, had come under attack by Indians. She felt guilty because she had been daydreaming while washing the dishes, so she hadn't been aware of what was occurring until too late. When she saw, she quickly wiped her hands and headed outside, but her small homestead was already overrun with Indians and everyone there was killed—lastly herself. Now, in her ghostly condition, she just wanted to return her home to its rightful order and finish her dishes!

At this time, Kevin and Corey returned, and we five third-dimension life forms went inside the house. First, we went to the kitchen and psychically helped the woman in plaid wash and stack her dishes, conveying to her the energy of a task at last completed. In response, she sighed and disappeared into the light—giving us all a sense of peaceful completeness.

Then we discussed the picnic grove situation. Although we had cleared the spirits that had been in the grove when we'd arrived, we explained to the couple that the location was a "rest stop" in the spirit world. They would therefore have to occasionally clear new "picnickers." They agreed to this and later told us that they had to do this every few weeks.

A key nodal point on the back side of the house, along the ley line, was the location of a fire pit the couple had recently built. Along that ley line there were a number of other active nodal points, along with another portal refugee from a nearby construction site. We came back later to assist with these issues.

LESSONS

Kevin and Corey's spiritual work helped bring many subtle frequencies more easily into the human perceptual range; thus, interdimensional interactions were significantly increasing at their newly purchased site. Because they were aware practitioners, they could sense an increase in spirit activity. But as this was not then their area of expertise, they called in colleagues who worked in these domains.

Because consciousness is multidimensional and all consciousness exists simultaneously above local time/space,[5] what one practitioner sees in an area may not be the same as what another sees. Practitioners work with specific families of guides and guardians in relationships in which they become accustomed to particular ways of dealing with existence. When practitioners from different disciplines work together, an end goal is accomplished via consensus. The practitioners need to be in harmony with one another so that one discipline does not override the findings of another.

Interdimensional communicators are often needed to assist ghosts in accomplishing what they perceive to be their final task—whether it is conveying a message to a loved one or washing the dishes. People will often see a ghost repeating a task as they struggle to master the situation; when the human steps in to help, the ghost is greatly relieved. As I mentioned in the introduction, working with a ghost is different from observing an energy break off, where the image keeps repeating the same action with no variation and does not interact with the observer. A break off is not a full spirit, but a portion of vital energy left behind in a traumatic situation. It cannot be worked with but instead needs to be dissolved.

Whether working with other practitioners or internally with their own team, energy practitioners may need to return several times to a site, to peel the layers of the onion and deal with a hierarchical list of issues resident in that specific time/space continuum.

When I start a clearing, I specify with the client exactly what aspect of the situation he or she wants help with first, so that we can focus on, or at least include, that issue. Very often, however, as soon as I arrive, the resident energies of the situation come forward to air their side of the story and their grievances with the humans who had requested my assistance. I often feel as if I am back at the United Nations, where I worked years ago!

EXERCISE

It is always good to prepare ahead of time for your own transition. What is it you expect will occur, and how are you going to be prepared to move forward to the highest possible plane of consciousness? I always remember how the great pacifist reformer Gandhi prepared himself for death. He prayed that his last words and thoughts would be of God so that at death he would be connected to that energy and travel that line of light back to source. It has been reported that when he was assassinated, Ghandi's last word was "God!"

Your intent creates a cord of consciousness to the higher worlds of spirit—not only in regard to death, but in regard to every action of your life.

Sit silently. Begin to review your life in areas of action. What is your intent in your action? Do you truly want to connect to the highest ideals? You may feel trapped by circumstances on earth. However, by consciously connecting to a higher energy, you are placing into work an energy that will eventually manifest on earth. Start committing to representing that higher energy. For a while you may not see a change, but watch—the changes do eventually evolve into place! They may not be as you want them to be right now, for cosmic energies need to find an appropriate way of descent, but if you will let them manifest as they wish, you will find you are happier. A good mantra used by many spiritual people is directed to source and is based on the teachings of Christ: "Not my will but Thy Will." Alignment with universal will always achieves the highest goal, whether it is on earth or in your own transition back to the worlds of spirit.

MAFIA HIT MAN

The age thirty-something Mafioso ghost was pacing about in the woods, watching the nature preserve path and studying every passerby. He was angry and bitter, waiting for his "friend."

More than half a century ago, the man and his "friend" had been visiting what was then a private estate owned by a sociable judge who, it was rumored, had ties to the Chicago Mafia. And, as was their wont on such occasions, the two Mafiosos had gone for a walk through the estate woods. However, this time his "friend" had orders to kill. When they had reached this spot, the colleague pulled a gun, shot the Mafioso, and buried him.

In life, the ghost had believed one simply stopped existing after death, but here he was—therefore he must be still alive. So he had been stalking the fence line ever since, waiting for the other man to come by so that he could exact revenge. In the blue-grey ghost world, time does not exist as it does in our world, and fifty years ago to that Mafioso seemed like only yesterday.

This is a dilemma for many ghosts. If their religion or understanding does not allow for life after death, but after death they are aware they still exist, they reason they must not be dead! So instead of looking for a way out of their situation, they attempt to continue on as they did when they were alive—a futile task, because they no longer have a physical form.

Over time, this ghost's restless stalking had imbued this section of the woods with a feeling of dark dread and ominous threat. On my occasional walks in this preserve, I had felt this dark energy and had always hurried past it. But this time I decided to stand and locate where the feeling came from. Caution as well as assessing your own capacities is always advisable when doing energy work. As I was fairly new at that time to this type of perception, and the ghost's energy was so dark, I decided it would not be wise for me to intervene. I continued on, and in my walks there afterward simply invoked angelic protection and passed by.

Interestingly, during my visit with Kevin and Corey and the prairie ghost, recounted in a previous story, my colleague Jody asked me to show her some places of energetic interest. So Jody, Cynthia, and I took an outing to this preserve. We happily explored vortexes, rock spirits, and water spirits, and eventually ended up in the dark woodland area. I explained the situation with the Mafioso to my colleagues and suggested that together the three of us might be of assistance. Jody is a "kick-butt" interdimensional energy worker who likes challenges, and here was one that intrigued her. She took a deep breath and said, "Let's go to it!"

I called the spirit to appear, and he did. We explained the situation to the spirit, and his awareness of what had occurred gradually dawned. Like a rejected shawl, he sloughed off his bitterness; he was now ready to move on. The three of us held loving, tight space, and Jody prepared to help the spirit cross over.

But the spirit surprised me. He could not go, he told me, without also assisting the twelve-year-old girl spirit he had befriended and was protecting. She would be all alone if he left without her! She was off playing somewhere, and he needed to locate her. He disappeared instantly.

Not hearing this conversation, Jody thought he had simply rejected help, which in her work meant the matter was closed. So she and Cynthia started walking ahead, moving into solid third-dimensional consciousness and chatting with each other. I lingered a moment and saw the man reappear, shielding the young girl with an arm. "We're ready," he said.

I called to my friends, but they were too far away to hear. I hurried after them, trying to get their attention, as the two spirits stayed with me, the man trying to keep my attention on their issue.

"We're ready," he kept saying, growing more agitated as we moved toward the end of his territory. (Ghosts usually have a certain parameter of territory in which they remain, and once you move beyond it, you leave the ghost behind.) As we approached the outer edge, his agitation at our leaving became so strong that I shouted, "Please stop! Come back!" Jody and Cynthia heard me and returned.

There was a stand of briar bushes right where we all now stood, and the man said this would be an excellent place to transition from. Briar bushes are excellent places to drop negative energy: they slurp it up, serving as a vacuum for a piece of land—a very appropriate place for the Mafioso.

Jody paused, squared her shoulders, and walked into the briar bush. The man and the child also headed into that space. Cynthia and I held space while Jody called on her guides to transition the spirits, and in an opening of white light, as the two left, a deep feeling of peace and gratitude wafted over the three of us.

That was the end of the ominous presence in this area of the preserve. However, several stands of trees where he had often stood to scout for his "friend's" return and some ley lines linking them held remnants of that dark energy for a long time. It was not until three years later that the area rebalanced itself. It now feels very pleasant and light.

Lessons

As described above, certain ghosts remain in an area because their particular cultural tradition states that everything ends with death: there is nothing after it. But when these individuals "die," they are still aware of themselves as existing. Therefore, they reason, they cannot be dead. Because they are not dead, they reason they will be able to complete a specific action they failed to accomplish while alive, and they stay to do so.

In the case of the Mafioso, his protection of the young girl spirit became his own path of redemption, transforming him enough so that he could transition on. It also gave him a reason to transition—to help her go to the light—a positive energy that was stronger than his old desire for revenge.

Spirits can remain in this monochromatic blue-grey in-between world for decades or centuries before they gradually begin to realize that something is amiss. But even when this occurs, they sometimes cannot find a way out.

Very often the interdimensional communicator can link to such a ghost's personal frequency and explain the situation to the spirit. This helps the confused spirit understand what is occurring. When the interdimensional communicator offers to show the spirit where a doorway out is located, the spirit gladly accepts, tired of its current experiences, and transitions to the light.

In the situation of the Mafioso, the ghost's energy was very dark as a result of his acts while on earth, so identifying with his consciousness to help send him on was not a pleasant action to anticipate. It is a good policy for interdimensional communicators, in consultation with our guides, to clearly assess the magnitude of a situation as well as our groups' current capacities. We can decide not to go in until we and our guides are in agreement that the situation has been correctly set up for positive results. In the Mafioso situation, which occurred when I was just beginning this work, I needed to bring in colleagues who were more experienced in such matters—some to hold positive energy while others went in through our protected force to correct the negative energy.

The Ghost Cat

Elizabeth was an attractive, energetic, seventy-year-old widow, devoted to her children and still, eleven years after his passing, deeply devoted to her late husband. She was not the kind of woman who liked to be by herself.

I hired Elizabeth to assist me in my company office. One day she asked me to assist her. "There is a spirit kitten who climbs into bed with me on cold nights and snuggles at my feet. It is freaking me out! Can you please get the cat to leave?" She said other people had tried to do this for her but had not succeeded.

We sat together and focused on the situation, and I connected with the spirit of a very sweet young kitten—a wild one who had frozen to death one cold winter's night. I sent the kitten into the light.

Each of the next two days, when Elizabeth came to work, she reported no kitten in her bed. But the third night, the kitten was back. She said I had not done any better than the psychics she had gone to!

I pondered this for a while. "Do you want the kitten to go?" I asked.

Elizabeth looked at me sheepishly. "No. I like the kitten," she admitted. "She keeps me company on the cold winter nights."

"Well, then," I explained gently, "there is really nothing further any of us can do. No matter how many times we send the kitten into the light, if you call it back before it has fully transitioned, it will return."

LESSONS

If a spirit is attached psychically or vitally to some person or place, that issue must be addressed first. That energy needs to be psychically cut and cauterized so that it does not pull back on the spirit to remain. People who are receiving help in this matter need to be very careful for the next three days. They should work very hard not to think about the spirit. If they do, they should immediately mentally encourage the spirit to continue its journey toward its rest in the realm of the light; then consciously stop thinking about the situation. After three days, spirits have usually transitioned far enough from the earth frequencies so that they can keep going forward on their own.

If a person wants to keep a spirit near them and the tie is strong, it is hard to help the spirit to leave. It is always better for everyone to help a life form transition on into the light. Before this transition, the spirit lives in a blue-grey in-between world, is confused, and is in need of help. Once the spirit transitions, the soul returns to the light. From this point, if the soul wishes to, it can come back to the person still on earth and offer true support from the realm of the light. Of course, it is also possible the soul has other adventures it wishes to now experience and does not want to come back and assist the human, especially if that situation had been filled with discord while both were on earth or if the human needs to learn to resolve his or her issues in another way. That is a chance the human must take.

THE NOVENA

Vicki and her eleven-year-old daughter Jessie were having considerable difficulties. Their home had belonged to Vicki's parents who had recently died. The father's ghost was there and bothering them. He had been abusive during his life and continued to be intrusive in death. In the winter they would often hear his footsteps walk up to the front door and the sound of a shovel clearing snow—only it had not snowed outside. They often felt his presence near the fireplace where he'd liked to sit.

Wanting to move, Vicki had called in a real estate agent who told her she would not be able to sell the house until it was cleaned up. All the parents' clothes were still in the bureaus and closets; Vicki and Jessie's belongings were piled in stacks along the walls. In this obvious disaster zone, it was evident that Vicki was having a very difficult time breaking free from the still-present energy of her father.

Vicki called me in for assistance. I checked out the house and found clear lines of energy from the father and mother still present throughout—in places where they had moved from room to room. The mother had crossed over, but the father had not. There were no other spirits around.

Vicki and I discussed another potential difficulty. Although Vicki wanted desperately to move, they were located in a very good school system, and Jessie wanted to stay because she had recently made very nice friends at school. Since the discussions about a move had begun, poltergeist activity had started occurring, with items flying off shelves in the kitchen, including knives.

"Occasionally," I explained, "when a young girl is just entering puberty, the bodily changes are sometimes accompanied by turbulent energy changes. There are latent subtle energetic capacities inside the child that pop open, uncontrolled, releasing a charge of energy, and then subsiding. When a pubescent girl is unhappy, the turbulence increases. Is there something that Jessie really, really wants that a move would enable her to have?" I asked.

"Jessie really wants a dog," Vicki replied, "but there isn't room here. There would be room if we moved to the country."

We discussed the issue with Jessie. With the prospect of a dog, she became more enthusiastic about the move, but she was still upset by the presence of her grandfather and the smell of stale smoke that accompanied him.

The three of us sat down together while I set space and then contacted the grandfather. He was indeed an old grouch! But he also had his own story. With a sanctimonious tone, he explained, "When I died, I understood how badly I had treated my family. I want to make amends! This is why I have stayed on, first to protect my wife, and now my daughter and granddaughter."

The sanctimonious tone did not ring true to me, nor did his story, especially since Vicki had told me that the two of them had never gotten along. There was something the old man was hiding. With a little more probing from me, he confessed. The real reason he stayed, he said, was because he was afraid of where he would go when he passed through the portal of death.

"I haven't been a good man," he said. "I've done many bad and unkind things." He spoke with anguish. "My priest always said such behavior is sinful and will send a person to hell! I don't want to go to hell!"

"Let's look at this in another way," I told him. "Is there anything that will help you receive a reprieve so you can exit in the other direction?" It is important to understand from the spirit's perspective what is needed; they have their own knowledge of what will work in their particular situation.

The grandfather paused and seemed to be consulting someone. Then he replied, "Yes. My daughter could say a novena for me—for nine days—and then my soul will be purified and can go to heaven instead of to hell. She can purchase a novena at the church, but she has to say it herself, not have the priest say it."

In looking at his response, I saw that it was necessary for Vicki to forgive her father, and in doing so, to release him; this would come from her reciting the novena herself.

I explained the solution to Vicki, and although she was no longer a churchgoer, she agreed to do it.

About two weeks later, Vicki called me. She was very distraught. "I purchased the novena and said it, and my father disappeared from the house, but he has come back the last few nights." She blamed him and me for the novena not working as promised.

I considered this, along with Vicki's penchant for not following through. "Did you complete the nine days as requested?" I asked.

She paused and was very sheepish. "I did four days, and he disappeared. So I stopped."

I explained that when something as serious as this is taking place and instructions have been very clearly given, the instructions must be followed or the desired result cannot occur. Her father had started to pass into the light, but had not been able to fully transition because she had stopped the clearing process too soon.

Vicki went back and started the novena over again. Three weeks later she called me with an update. "I completed the prayer cycle, and my father is gone," she said with real joy.

Vicki was now able to take action in the family home, packing and giving all her parents' clothes to charity. About six months later, she called to let me know that she had sold the house, purchased a lovely one in a more country setting, and that weekend she and her daughter were getting a dog.

Lessons

When you are working in other dimensions, you have to allow for different rules that prevail in different worlds. If you want to affect a specific situation, you can confer with the energies involved who can explain to you what needs to be done in their world to correct the issue. If you do as requested, then the guardians with whom you are working can assure success.

But if you second guess them or become lazy and fail to complete the process, then not only is success not assured, you can actually create a more difficult situation for yourself. The half-finished process will cause the energies to morph into something new. They may dig into a new and deeper aspect of the energy field where they will be harder to dislodge than when you caught them by surprise in a relatively open field.

With regard to Jessie, it is very sad that in our Western culture we do not train talented youths about their extended capacities and the various dimensions that exist in the universe. In a different culture, Jessie's capacities would have been spotted long ago, and she would have been trained to responsibly work with her extended abilities. Instead, she and other such children are told their capacities are not real; should they think they are experiencing something, they must consider the experience unnatural, sinful, evil, or a sign of personal madness. Trying to mandate that people reject what is occurring to them causes so much conflict that this alone can drive a person crazy!

If you know of any youths experiencing extended perception, look around in your area or on the Internet for groups working with Crystals, Indigoes, and Rainbow children. In the Geneva, Illinois, area, Crystal Life Technology hosts the Blue Papaya youth group.

THE HAUNTED HOTEL

The grand old Stanley Hotel in Estes Park, Colorado, is known as the second most haunted hotel in America—surpassed only by a New Orleans hotel where such activity increased after Hurricane Katrina.

I unexpectedly discovered the Stanley Hotel's very active energy when, on a nature photography shoot in Estes Park, I booked a night in the hotel simply because it had an online special. On check-in, looking at me strangely, the clerk asked if I preferred a room in the old part of the hotel. Because she seemed to be directing me to it, I said yes. Quaint would be nice, I thought.

Upstairs in the room, I sensed some energies, but that is usual for me when I travel, and I thought nothing of it. I opened the window. Despite its good strong fit, it slammed shut three times within fifteen minutes. This caught my attention, but I'd had a busy week at a show, and I bluntly requested that all energies please leave me alone. I needed to rest. I was starting to unpack when what sounded like a tour stopped outside my door. Curious, I opened the door to discover a guide explaining to a crowd of tourists that this was the most haunted floor of the hotel. She was leading a ghost tour!

Well, of course I had to take the tour and I changed my schedule accordingly. It turned out this was the hotel where Stephen King had stayed and that had inspired his book *The Shining*. The resident spirits included a staid old housekeeper who would settle down in bed to separate a couple if they were not married; the attentive, celebrity-loving, hospitable wife of the original owner; a lecherous former landowner who could still, even in ghost form, steal jewelry right off the hand of the wearer; a grumpy alcoholic caretaker; and a number of children, maid servants, and other ghosts. These had all been seen by numerous guests and employees.

The guide told us that a Colorado university professor had done a scientific study of the hotel and produced a paper about what he called the Stanley Effect. The guide said the professor believed the combination of minerals on which the hotel was built—limestone, quartz, and pyrite— plus the electrical power plant situated at a lake nearby, augmented the frequency at which paranormal events are brought into the human energy range. In essence, the combined elements were connecting the two frequency worlds, human and spirit, and amped up the ability of the ghost realm to affect the physical realm.

Often some of the ghosts would join the tour and that happened on mine. I smelled old-fashioned rosewater, which the guide explained was the ghost wife's favorite scent. Then I saw the ghost standing by the tour director at the entrance to a haunted bedroom. She was acknowledging me in a friendly manner, possibly because I was someone "important" in that particular group, being an author. When the group went inside the bedroom, I happened to stand behind the bed. I watched with interest as the friendly ghost came in toward me and sat down on the bed, right in front of me, leaving a depression from her rump and a scent of rosewater in the air. The tour guide was also aware of this occurrence and pointed it out to the group.

The tour ended on my floor, and I went back to my room, ready to take a brief nap. However, the ghost and her rosewater scent came in with me. By now I had been consciously working with spirits for many years. I knew how to turn off the ability to see them and turn the ability back on. The tour had provided me with the opportunity to experience the ghosts, and now I just wanted to sleep! So I grumpily thanked the ghost for her hospitality but asked if she would please leave and take her friends with her. There was a slight pause and then the ghost replied politely, "Well, all right, dear, I just wanted to make sure you were comfortable!" I replied I was, thanked her again, and she and all her friends left.

Lessons

The energetic base of an area affects the types of life forms that will be most easily experienced. It sets a particular band of energy as the predominant field. Other energies moving into the space are affected and find that the course of least resistance is to coordinate or harmonize with the dominant energies. At this particular location, ghosts predominate. But in other areas of Estes Park, stone energies predominate and, in fact, this is the reason I was there. I wanted to capture better photographs of my stone friends whom I had come to know and love on previous trips. (You can see my stone friend photos in the story "Grandfather Rock" in chapter 4.)

Regarding my request that the spirit leave my room, it is useful to understand that we all—both ghosts and humans—have free-will rights. The ghost was a hospitable host, and when I exerted my free-will right to get a good rest, she responded with politeness and arranged for it to occur.

People have said to me, "Your practice involves helping spirits cross over. Why didn't you send all these folks to the light? Why did you leave them there?"

What to do about ghosts varies with every situation. One needs to consider why the ghost is there, what humans have done to change the original situation, and how the ghost and the situation have evolved.

In this case, the environment itself was holding the spirits in place, and unless that environment was altered, one batch of ghosts could be sent over only to have another set take their place.

Then there is the fact that some ghosts feel a great deal of responsibility for a particular location and take on the task of guardian of place.

Sometimes a ghost inhabits an inn or hotel and is part of the commercial success of the establishment, and for this reason the owner does not wish the situation to change. A little interdimensional social group forms at the site!

Friendly ghosts and hostile spirits are different. If a hostile spirit is bringing discord to an area, it is useful to bring in someone to assess the situation, locate a solution, and send the spirit away.

• 2 •

Humans, Spirit Guides, and Thought Forms

FOLDS IN TIME

Three energy workers met together one bright spring weekend in Princeton, New Jersey. At that time, Doreen was helping human souls cross over, Lydia was working with nature spirits, and I was working with land energies.

As we headed out for a walk, Doreen announced, "We have a special spot to show you, but we're not going to tell you anything about it! We don't want you influenced by anything either of us have experienced there!"

A short trek through the woods brought us to a quiet spot with a small pond and a lemony-green wooded hillside fringed by custom-built houses, some still under construction. The patch of land we were headed to, in the top middle of this scene, was undeveloped. We walked up the hill, and my friends paused at the top. In front of us was a forest filled with shimmering golden light. And there, nestled into the flat woodland rise just a notch above third-dimensional frequency, was a Pioneer-era Native American village. Children in buckskins were laughing and playing in the center of the circle. They were vibrantly alive, yet at the same time were not moving. The scene faded from view and a new scene appeared: pioneer-era soldiers in dark blue coats riding through the same area on horseback, aware of nothing but woodlands all around.

The three of us discussed this. On previous visits, both Doreen and Lydia had seen the Native American village and the children but they could not fathom what was occurring. Doreen knew these were not "lost" souls in the usual sense—that is, departed souls who needed help transitioning to the light. Lydia knew they were not inner earth beings who needed assistance.

They said it was my turn to explore the site using my modalities. So, moving into a full body-dowsing, information-seeking mode, I accepted their friendly challenge and began walking about the area, inwardly scanning for the frequency of consciousness where this story lived. There were three large vortexes in the space: one for the village, another to the far right, and a third behind the village. Each was, in the manner of a holding field,[6] in a circle. The village area was clearly suspended in time and space[7] but did not contain the source of the situation. We walked far enough toward the vortex on the right to ascertain that the story, while connected, also did not originate there, and the energy was not particularly pleasant. So we continued to the vortex at the rear. The energy coming from this area was much stronger. It was, however, surrounded by a ring of negative energy; we felt it strongly repelling us.

My inner team now spoke, telling me the answer was in this area. They suggested we check out the circle. When I told my friends, they were reluctant to do so because, in general, it isn't wise to enter into any protected circle without first comprehending, or receiving permission, from the energies inside. Rechecking with my colleagues, they repeated—louder this time—"Go in, it's safe; we're with you."

My arrangement with my guides is that I trust their judgment in such matters, so I did as requested and stepped inside the vortex. What a surprise! The circle was filled not with dark energies but with holiness and protection. "Wow," I told my friends, "you have to come feel this!"

My friends now entered and experienced this for themselves, each in her own way. Meanwhile, my guides had me spinning my inner grid dials so that I could identify with the precise frequency of the story—which emerged slowly, like an animal awakening from a long sleep. However, what was taking form was so strange that I found myself unable to accept it with an open heart and trusting mind. I shut down. I turned off the capabilities to "know," and we returned home.

The following day I woke up with a strong feeling that we needed to return to the site. There was something there that required assistance. I asked my friends to walk back there, but Doreen had an unexpected call to assist one of her interior design clients and had to leave for a few hours, and Lydia had broken some bones in her right foot two nights before, and yesterday's walk had caused it to swell and throb with pain. We decided it would be best for her to stay at the house, resting her foot and holding the space from outside the vortex, and I would go on alone.

It was a sunny, quiet, windless day. Retracing my steps through the woods, I came to the hill, saw the village, saw the children, saw the soldiers, and proceeded on to the sacred circle. Again, I paused at its perimeter.

This was going to be an unusual story, and my colleagues told me that the guardians of the vortex were giving us a choice: we could leave, or, if I wanted my team to help resolve the story, we could move inside the vortex. The energy in this announcement was detached, as it always is when I work with my inner colleagues. This is a free-will universe, and we all have a choice about our own decisions. I asked my inner colleagues if they were comfortable going forward. Receiving assurance that they could call in from other dimensions whatever assistance was needed, I stepped inside the vortex.

This time, the guardian energies of the circle were willingly communicating with me and my inner colleagues. They pointed out a large constructed circle of stones half buried by centuries of woodland leaves. Tall trees, hundreds of years old, had grown up over many of the stones, curling their roots around them and continuing down into the ground. The sense of conscious protection and disguise was very strong.

These guardians directed my attention to a flat altar-shaped stone, hidden from casual sight by woodland debris, set near the circle edge on the side that bordered the village. "Sit here," they advised me, "so you can more easily identify with the story hidden here. This is the seat of the holy person from whom this energy is emanating."

"Wouldn't sitting here be a sacrilege?" I queried inwardly.

"Ask permission, with humility," the guardians replied.

I did, and it was granted.

I sat down and entered into a scanning, meditative reverie. As often happens to me, the story that began unfolding contained consciousness concepts I was not then aware of. For me, as for many energy workers, service is simultaneous learning, assisting, accepting, becoming, and being.

I was shown that during the pioneer era a village of peaceful Native Americans lived on this site. There was growing discord in the area, with wars between competing factions, including Native American tribes on both sides as well as European settlers from various countries on both sides. The tribe that lived here wished to exist in peace with all, but it was becoming more difficult, and violence was coming nearer. The most troublesome group in the situation was another tribe whose people had long been enemies of the village's tribal nation; therefore they were working with the European pioneers to eliminate their tribal enemies. I was shown the marauders, who had a long central mane of hair with short or shaved sides, such as some Algonquins and Iroquois, but their specific name was not shown to me.

The medicine man of the tribe was old, wise, and very advanced in Native ways. He knew how to transmute energy. He understood about the "rip tide" areas between dimensions where energy and objects could be stored—"parked" or "filed" for later retrieval, like books in a library. The chief of the village was a middle-aged man, a friend and protégée of the medicine man. Through a village-wide decision-making process, the following was decided:

If the village was about to be attacked, the medicine man would go outside the village, sit on his medicine seat, and connect to the chief, who would sit in his home inside the village. The medicine man was to elevate the village into a frequency between dimensions, parking it there until the danger was passed.[8] He would maintain a cord, or chain, or link, to the village via the chief. When the danger was gone, he would connect to the chief, and together they would bring the village back into the third-dimension frequencies. During this time, a young village boy, the medicine man's acolyte, would tend to the old man's needs, with food and warm clothing.

This interdimensional parking occurred several times, quite successfully. Then, one day, during the early winter, when a light snow was covering the ground like white spots on a tawny wildcat's back, raiders approached the village. The medicine man became aware of this, but no one else saw. The little boy was still inside the village, intent in his play with other village children.

The medicine man tried with increasing forcefulness to break through and contact the young boy, who ignored the call in the intensity of play. The intensity of the medicine man's call rendered that part of the village particularly strong in energy, which was why my friends and I had seen it so clearly.

Finally, the medicine man had no choice but to proceed alone and he sent the village into its interdimensional parking space.

The marauders unfortunately chose to camp in what was now the second darker vortex area.

It was cold, and without the child providing the simple physical care that had been his duty, the medicine man had two choices. He could release the village from its safe parking space back into the third dimension, which would mean certain slaughter for himself and his village. Or he could remain in place and, in the little time he had left before he froze to death, he could weave a stout cord, anchoring the village in that other dimension in which it was now hidden. The medicine man chose the latter option, weaving his masterpiece: a net of energy that anchored the village in the rip area, attached by energetic cords to the very stones of the earth. He triangulated the energy lock—a very powerful force—by connecting the village to the marauders' area and to his area.

It would now have to wait for some future time for all to be released: if not sooner, then at the end of the age earth was now in.

Figure 2.1. The location of the protected Native American village.

Figure 2.2. The location of the marauders' camp.

Figure 2.3. The medicine man's vortex, with trees falling down in line with his focus. His seat was in the point toward the left, facing his village. Notice the tree growing over a rock, to the right, with other trees falling in line with its energy; there is a thought form there; see close-up in Figure 2.7.

Figure 2.4. The medicine man's seat. He sat on the lower part of the rock to the right and placed his ritual objects on the raised ledge to the left; the protected village is to the left of that. Note the line of trees that have fallen in line with his focus. Unlike other Native American power spots where the energies have asked me to clean up the sacred spot (see "Grandfather Rock" story, chapter 4), here the energies asked me to leave the seat uncleared to protect it from those walking along the trail nearby.

Figure 2.5. Trees as they have fallen in line with the focused intent of the medicine man, whose seat is within the *V* at the center of the photo, looking toward the village at the left.

Figure 2.6. View from the medicine man's circle of energy, looking toward the village. Notice the clear demarcation of energy between the medicine man's circle of energy, with trees falling along its outer edge, and the area he was protecting, which is filled with soft grass.

Figure 2.7. One of the trees that grew up in the medicine man's circle of energy. It wrapped around various of the rocks that circled his ceremonial space. Note the thought form he placed there (circled). This is the tree to the right of the vortex shown previously.

Some two hundred years later, the three vortexes were still together, suspended in time. The chief was still inside his home, suspended while smoking his pipe, unaware that anything was wrong.

The vision ended. I sat in silence, taking in what was at the time a story so bizarre, I could not possibly have imagined it—an option I carefully considered.

"Well," I said inwardly to my guides and their sources. "This is quite a story. And just what are we to do about this?"

"Would you like us to help?" they asked.

"Of course," I replied, more from the obligation implied in their question than from any real desire to get involved. "But this is a situation unlike

Figure 2.8. Another thought form, placed over another rock in the circle and where another tree grew in the energy field.

anything I've ever encountered. I have no idea what to do. We can create more problems than we solve."

I thought a moment, then asked hopefully, "Can't we just leave them there? It is very peaceful where they are. Eventually, when this age is over, which is soon, they will come back down."

A long inner discussion ensued. My guides explained: "The souls in the village are suspended in time. That means they're losing their opportunity to learn and evolve. Until these souls are found, the soul families involved will be delayed in their group effort to fully master consciousness. The situation is delaying each soul group's evolutionary process."

Because these life forms, with their inner guides, were suspended between dimensions, their soul families could not find them. It would cause too many complications to bring the village back down into the third dimension, now operating in the twenty-first century. It was too complicated for me and my team to try to reconnect each person with their own soul family. Together, we decided that the best course of action was for my guides to contact the chief's soul family, alert them as to where he was, and together he and his guides and soul family could start the reclamation process.

After we agreed on this course of action, I sat quietly in meditation until my guides returned, reporting they had contacted the chief's soul family. I then was privileged to inwardly watch as contact was made. The chief gently "came to," as if from a short reverie, finished pulling on his peace pipe, sending up a wisp of smoke, and his soul family began to brief him on what had occurred. He was very wise, thoughtful, brave, quiet, and measured as his soul family spoke with him. He nodded agreement, and the reclamation of the suspended life forms in all three vortexes began.

Our work was done, and we closed the window of sight on this story.

After pausing a few moments to collect myself, I walked back to Doreen's home. There, sitting with her leg propped up, was Lydia.

"You helped them," she said. We were both feeling very peaceful.

"Yes," I replied, "how did you know?"

"Just a bit longer than it would have taken you to walk back," Lydia said, "a sudden gust of wind rushed through here, from your direction. It was not the weather; there has not been a breath of wind all day. I felt it come from a release of energy. Then a white owl, my totem, suddenly appeared and landed in the pine tree right here and called out."

A few weeks later, my guides brought me news from the guides and soul families of the village members. All had now been located by their soul families and removed. The rescue was complete.

A bare six months later, on our next meeting in Princeton, Doreen, Lydia, and I hiked out to the site again. We were shocked: Gone was the shimmering light. Gone was the feeling of sanctity. Gone was the Native American village. And when we reached the sacred circle of that long-ago medicine man, we found a strange sight. One-third to one-half of the trees had fallen down, following the various lines of energy the medicine man had originally set up.

The feeling of peaceful protection was gone. Instead, we felt that the local ley lines, held back for so long outside that vortex, had rushed in, connecting and returning to their natural flow. It was now an ordinary woodland scene.

Lessons

Doreen moved from that area a short time later. After two years passed, I returned to check what had occurred since this event. The turmoil of the sudden change had calmed down. The photos in this chapter are from that visit, and show some of the original energy still present, as well as the physical land configurations. This type of land imprint occurs when a very strong energetic situation has occurred on a piece of land. This energetic imprint will stay for a certain amount of time before it dissipates and the resident energies of the area move in. A similar situation occurred in "Mafia Hit Man" (chapter 1).

An energy imprint, as well as still-living energies resulting from past events, can affect the energy of whatever is built in a particular space. This is one of the reasons why it is so valuable, before building on seemingly "raw" land, to perform a ceremony to clear the energies. Otherwise, those who move there will be affected by the previous use and not even be aware of it so that they can fix it.

While the protected village, the marauders' camp, and the medicine man's power circle were next to each other, their energies differed significantly. The land where the village had been suspended still retained the imprint of the medicine man's protection and was filled with light and soft green vegetation. The marauders' area, just across a present-day woodland path, was dark with greyed trees and dull light. The medicine man's circle had a core of softly lit, peaceful grass with a perimeter where energies had been wrestled for control. The medicine man's circle included his circle of stones, now overgrown by trees, where he had brought down cords of energy to anchor the village in the fold in time; the thought forms placed in each tree still visibly present; and the lines of trees that had grown over time and fallen in the same directions as the medicine man's focused intent.

Very often a serious situation evolves from a simple lack of conscious awareness or completion of a contract or duty. In this case, the child's failure to respond to the medicine man's call became the seemingly small duty ignored that brought a cascade of disasters.

MORE LESSONS

We humans see three-dimensionally because we have agreed to focus on that dimension. We have strengthened the grids to support this perception. But we can likewise choose to focus on other frequencies. These are also equally valid realms of existence.

We live in a very big universe, with many different life forms. It is difficult to comprehend the texture of this energy that resides everywhere at once. Therefore, energy workers almost always work with inner colleagues who help them to comprehend the complex mixing of forces they are sure to encounter. These colleagues work on their own, and they also know how to get appropriate interdimensional help to deal with whatever is at hand.

Some factors to consider: It is important for your team to be in agreement regarding any major project being undertaken. Be sure your team has permission to call in whatever assistance will be needed. It is never good to exclude some form with interest in the matter; battles often begin over territorial issues, so make sure you always invoke the highest good for all involved. At some point, all conflicting issues find a goal of common good, and this is what we are seeking to manifest for the form we are assisting.

The situation in this story was discussed among the various parties via interdimensional communication, which permits different life forms to understand one another. I experienced the story in a detached manner as it was being told. It is important to remember that emotional involvement dissipates the ability to see into the scene. Remote viewers practice this to an extreme extent and do not interact with what they are viewing. Energy workers get involved to change the situation but do not become involved emotionally.

When emotional involvement occurs, it can lead to the observer becoming trapped, energetically or physically, inside that field. This is what happens sometimes to people labeled as schizophrenic or unbalanced: they are having experiences in other times/spaces, but our culture does nothing to teach them how to secure the perimeters of different fields so that they are only experiencing one dimension at a time. Their emotional and mental distress in not understanding what is occurring compounds and creates problems of its own.

This kind of compounding distress also occurs when people are spontaneously transported into another dimension and return without understanding what has occurred. There are myriad "faery tales" about humans who wander into the faery world—a dimension close to our human one—and are so entranced that they never want to return to the grosser human world. Sometimes the faery rulers force them to return and the humans are often treated as "daft" or "touched" because they keep insisting to others that they have been to a place "ordinary" humans "know" does not exist. Sometimes the humans pine for faeryland so powerfully that the faeries have compassion for them and bring them back—in which case, the human world simply believes that the person has "disappeared!"

Interdimensional communication requires a learned ability to shift frequencies of perception. The key to this type of communication is an acceptance that all in the universe is alive and has one common source. Because all is of the same ultimate substance, perceiving and communicating with any form requires only a "simple" adjustment of frequency modulation, angle, and spin. We scan for the frequency on which the life form exists, then enter into this field and "talk" or "perceive."

EXERCISE

Schedule a quiet time when you will not be disturbed. Sit silently, and let your energies quiet down. Invoke protection. Draw a map of your home and property, and label it with the date. Contemplate the map. What cultures do you know or think preceded you in this area?

Now go for a walk, first around your home and then around your property. Do you see evidence of special energies anywhere? Trees or rocks with unusual formations? Changes in light? A sense of a presence of some life form?

It was said by the "sleeping prophet" Edgar Cayce that as frequency refines, we will see evidence of past cultures all around us, always there but we just didn't see them before. Now that you are aware that such a situation could exist, start exploring right in your own home!

Any place you feel there is something different, mark it on your map. If you hear or sense a reason why, note that down as well.

Now go back to your quiet place, and contemplate what you have observed. Do this repeatedly for deeper and deeper understanding.

PHOTOGRAPHS

If you have a large yard, start here. If you don't, choose a local park or preserve that you really like and go there.

To get a good nature spirit image, you have to have the cooperation of the nature spirits themselves. These spirits exist in subtle space, and they can very easily dematerialize into nothingness or come forward to be photographed. So the very first thing to do is to stand respectfully at the start of your outing and humbly let the nature spirits know that you are here to assist them in their work. You want to show other humans that nature is alive and conscious. Stand quietly, and listen to their response. When and if they accept your offering, they will lead you to remarkable sites to photograph the energies. You must listen carefully, however, for at the start their voices are very soft and gentle. You may get the thought to turn left at the next dividing point instead of right as you usually go; listen and follow. They may tell you to stop at a specific location you always thought was particularly uninteresting. Stop. Look. Listen. They will very soon show you what is so special and how they have kept it hidden from humans, for self-preservation—like the medicine man's ring of rocks and his personal altar, in the preceding story.

Sometimes you won't see anything, but should the spirits ask you to photograph, stop, listen, adjust, identify, and shoot.

When you are done and are leaving, stop to thank the nature spirits for their assistance.

When you can, download the photos into the computer. If you are using a film camera, have the images scanned onto a disk that you can transfer to your computer. Now comes the tricky part. You may very well see nothing in a photo and wonder why you took it. Ask the energies of that spot why—what was so special? They may well lead you to a tiny area of the photo and ask you to move in close, and there you may find an image of some very special energy.

If you take forty photos and only one has something of interest, that is one more than you had before. One good photo every several outings adds up over time!

Lastly, do not delete any of the photos you just took. Save them in a file with the date and location. Several months or years from now, as you become more experienced, you can go back to these photos. Your focus on nature spirit energy will have refined, and often people discover that they have some very interesting images they have simply been too inexperienced to recognize! Also, the nature spirits may have originally led you to a specific image they wanted known, whereas later, other images can be seen, too.

GUARDIAN OF THE SPRING

A number of years ago, a developer bought a large parcel of land that was behind our family's secluded New Hampshire getaway and began constructing an upscale housing development. Like most Westerners, feeling that this was simply empty land, the builders merrily carved up plots, plowed down trees, and built homes.

I didn't go there often, but a short time after some new houses were built in this area, I visited and had frightening dreams. I felt some sort of terrifying creature stalking about in the woods, trying to approach me. I felt defenseless while unconscious, so I began sleeping with various images and prayers of protection.

By the time of my next visit, a few years later, I was immersed in learning about subtle land clearing. My first night there, I was aware that this creature was still around and was still trying to approach me. This time I sat down quietly, focused on the energy, and drew the form. It was a composite animal, walking on two legs, with a wolf head, claws, and hooves. I didn't know what to do about the situation, but at least I knew what the creature looked like. I continued sleeping with various items of protection and chanting.

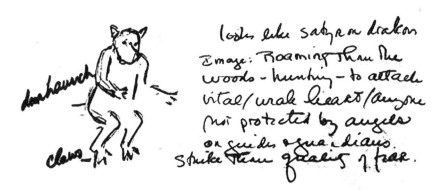

Figure 2.9. The notes around this image say: "Looks like satyr or drakon. Image: Roaming thru the woods—hunting—to attack vital/weak heart/anyone not protected by angels or guides and guardians. Strike through quality of fear." And beside the figure: "deer haunch," "claws" (I used "like" because I was comparing the life form to a satyr, a combined life form whose lower body is that of a four-footed goat who walks upright, and to a drakon who is an extraterrestrial life form.)

The following winter I took initiation with Randall, a master teacher within the Native American and Mayan traditions. In the course of his teachings, he touched on the thought forms placed in sacred locations by Native American medicine people to protect their sites from intruders. These thought forms were intended to stay until they were retrieved by the medicine person who had put them in place. However, as Randall explained, no one had foreseen the cultural shift that was coming to our world, the dissolution of the Native American culture, and the lack of awareness of the superseding white culture.

Many current land problems and human health issues are the result of homeowners and communities unknowingly building on a former culture's sacred sites. Sacred site situations are particularly resistant to a changing of their fields—more so than straight earth-energy geopathic fields.

During Randall's teachings, I started thinking about the animal form I'd seen at my family's summer home. The following day, I brought in my sketchbook and showed him my drawing of the being. Randall recognized the energy, because he had cleared various sites of similar forms, using a long, complex, energetically draining but ultimately effective set of ceremonies taught to him by Native American medicine people.

In discussing the situation with him, and thinking back over the known history of the cottage's area, I felt the following scenario must have occurred: There must have been a spring in the woods behind our summer place that had belonged to a local tribe. Some long-ago medicine person had placed this thought form there to protect the spring for his community. After the emigration to this area of European settlers, that indigenous community moved away with no one even remembering that a guardian spirit had been placed there. For many hundreds of years, the being had remained there, fulfilling its purpose, which was protection.

To truly protect the site and scare others away, the medicine person had made this being a fierce and fearful form—similar to the great and fierce dogs and gods that protect the entrances to Chinese and Tibetan temples. The thought form was to protect something necessary for the survival of this group—water. Thus, on a practical level, it was a form of dark light if you had no business being near the spring. It was a form of protective light if you were seeking to protect the site.

Randall explained that a problem with thought forms is that they are usually sent forth by a specific individual, with protective "codes" set in the energy field to prevent the forms from being dissolved or sent away by anyone but the person who first projected it. It is therefore dangerous to attempt to "dismantle" the thought form, unless you have serious training in the techniques.

In my situation, the thought form had been dislodged from the site it was created to protect. The site had most likely been destroyed during the construction period. And now the thought form was lost and wandering.

Because a thought form evolves by absorbing the energies of what is taking place around it, there is no way for energy workers to know ahead of time exactly what energy they are dealing with. Randall suggested I not approach the life form on my own; either leave it be or call in an expert.

However, when I checked with my own guides and guardians, they explained that our lineage does not work in the same way as Randall's. If I waited, the guides said, I would soon get more information on this situation.

The following summer I attended the annual convention of the American Society of Dowsers. (Dowsers know a great deal about the intricacies of working with land and they like to teach; learn more about this science at the ASD website, www.dowsers.org.) One evening I wandered into an open question session between the audience and the teachers onstage. Someone was asking a question about their land, and it inspired me to relate my own story and ask for the teachers' suggestions.

Everyone on the panel recommended that I not approach the thought form directly and that I be very cautious. That was as far as they would go on the subject in this open meeting. But after the meeting, two of the teachers—Benton Jordan (not his real name) and Marty Cain (the head of the dowsing school)—separately approached me with further suggestions. After ascertaining that I had a good working relationship with my inner guides and guardians, they each recommended distancing myself from direct contact with the energy involved and working through my guides. Beyond this, their two approaches diverged.

Benton stated that this energy form was potentially destructive in its origin and it should be approached from a "power over" defensive posture.[9] He recommended asking my guides to tell the thought form to leave the property and never return or the guides would confine it in a small black box about an inch wide for all eternity. These forms do not want to be imprisoned and therefore will leave.

While I was pondering this harsh methodology, Marty approached me. Marty is an experienced earth energy worker, known for her compassion. She has a good working relationship with the gnomes and other integral earth energies. Her approach was completely different, and it totally reshaped my approach to my own work.

"Oh," she said, "that poor, poor being. Just think how lost and alone it must be feeling. It has lost not only its home but also must feel like a failure: it failed to protect the site it was created to guard." She went on to explain, in gentle, communal fashion, that there was no way home for this being. And no one was acknowledging its existence or had any concern for it at all. When it found that I was aware of it, it kept approaching me for help.

Marty recommended I not approach the form directly, for it still might attack—because that was its job. She suggested I talk with my guides and ask them to please approach the being. I should request that my guides thank and acknowledge the thought form's long and faithful service. It had done its utmost to serve the consciousness for which it was formed. It was not its fault that the site had been destroyed. But now that the site was gone, the form could at last rest. We should ask it if it would like to join others of its kind—for some companionship—and go to the light for rest, resolution, and its own growth.

This approach made more sense to me, for it was in service to the light and to the earth's evolutionary growth.

When one goes above local time and space, one can be anywhere one projects oneself. So that night, in silence, I called together my guides to discuss the situation. They were in agreement about this solution and departed to contact the thought form. A while later, they reported to me that contact had been made and the thought form was considering what they'd said. It had not thought of itself in these terms before. A few days later, my guides told me the thought form had chosen to accept their offer and had gone to the light.

When I checked inwardly with the family home, the energy was gone. And on my next summer visit, the energetic change was evident and my nighttime sleep peaceful. Finally I broached the topic with my brother and sister-in-law as an interesting story. It turned out Eve had also been afraid of being alone there and had been surprised how comfortable she was feeling on this visit. My brother Chet, also a sensitive, had never felt any of this—probably because he was the "commander" of the land and the thought form avoided him!

Lesson

The base situation in this story can be found throughout the world— wherever construction is taking place without a prior sanctifying and clearing of the land energies or where there is no consultation with the other life forms involved in such a major transformative event. Since this experience, I have helped clear many energy-full sites where people's health and happiness are being seriously affected by spirits and energy forms. Our Western mainstream culture can offer the landowners no clue as to the real whys and wherefores of what they are experiencing on their property.

This was my first encounter with a thought form that had evolved, and at first I saw only its protective energy warning people to stay away. I subsequently began to understand that all life forms are beautiful to their own species. When we don't see their beauty, it is our shortcoming, not theirs. Once we identify with them and their reason for existence, we are more able to help resolve the issues that have brought their world and ours into conflict.

This situation also highlights the fact that, when doing this work, we must be bluntly honest about our own capacities. If we cannot handle the matter, we need to acknowledge this honestly and decide what approach to take so that we do not become victims. If we and our inner teams decide to proceed, we know that by the time we resolve the situation, the process has already started to make us more knowledgeable for the next time we encounter something similar.

EXERCISE

This is another land survey exercise. As before, start by locating a quiet place where you will not be disturbed. Have a piece of blank paper and a pencil with you. Sit silently and let your energies quiet down. Invoke protection.

Draw a diagram of your house and property as best you can—a rough estimate of the spaces. Bless your home and land. Thank it for protecting you and your family.

Now mentally take a walk around your home, both inside and out. Sense where there is a shift in energy: places you really like and places you are not fond of. In each of these locations, place a mark on the map: a + for liking, a – for disliking.

Select one place you particularly like. Identify with its energy. Bless it and offer it gratitude. Wait for it to respond to your outreach. Does it come with a feeling, a thought, an image? What is that energy like? How can you and it work to enhance the overall benefits of your home? Is there a task it needs performed? In what time frame?

When you have completed this query, offer gratitude to the spot, the home, and to your protecting energy, and return to normal consciousness.

If you agreed to perform some task for this area, remember to keep your promise.

You can repeat this task daily, each time choosing a + or a – location to inwardly connect to and adjust. A – location will offer suggestions, too. Listen to the suggestions and decide whether to proceed or to invoke your protecting guide and find a way to instead change its energies. If you locate a very hostile area, such as in the story above, wait. Don't do anything just yet. Take the issue to your protecting guides, ask them what to do, and wait for an answer which may take some time. Or locate an energy worker who can assist.

PHOTOGRAPHS

In the situation in this story, I roughly drew the energy that I "saw." In the old days, pre-camera era, many artists did just this: Goya in his *Night Dreams* series, Bosch in his grotesque landscapes of the mind, the many English painters who drew charming faeries, and artists who through the ages depicted cosmic gods and goddesses. While each situation was unique, each artist was watching energy, observing how it took physical form, and working with how to express that. The energy that was being watched could be bizarre, or cute, or full of power or love. There was an acknowledgment that something was present, and the artists were attempting to depict what they saw in that world. The observer could decide if it was imagination or a reality.

The new spirit photographers, as well as folks simply taking shots with digital cameras and getting "unexplainable" forms, are also presenting pictures of subtle life forms. When you begin to try to understand the situation, you become a spiritual scientist.

THE ROUNDTABLE OF THE HEART

Louise was an attractive young business executive with long black hair and deep dark brown eyes. She was a successful administrator, but her success was not bringing her happiness. She couldn't stop feeling that she needed to stop her current line of work and find a way to work in a more holistic field.

Louise made an appointment with me, stating she needed assistance from her guides but was having trouble contacting them. She was aware someone was trying to communicate with her; she would wake up in the morning with bits of disjointed information but couldn't establish direct communication.

Louise arrived for her consultation on a sparkling, snowy winter day and settled in to work on her issue. The first thing we did was to "set space" so that there was a merkabah of clear energy surrounding both of us. This gave us a place to begin the communication process.

Turning on my empathic abilities, I "observed" what was occurring, which turned out to be a fairly common situation at the time in Midwestern suburban Chicago. There was a block—a line of energy—about four inches above Louise's head. This line of energy was an intelligent frequency whose message was: "There are no such things as guides and guardian angels! Be sensible, work hard, and accept responsibility for your own decisions."

Louise's guides and angels were very actively seeking to communicate with her and were trying their best to bridge this blockage. Below this line, Louise was trying to reach up to see these life forms but also could not bridge the blockage.

"Louise," I asked, "do you have a ringing in one ear?"

Surprised, she replied, "Yes! Sometimes it's worse than other times!"

When we set out to clarify the cause of this condition, we learned that it was occurring because Louise was continually calling for assistance from her guides who were trying to respond but were not fully succeeding. The guides were responding on a different frequency than Louise was working from. They needed to adjust their pitch. In addition, Louise was blocking their response, thinking what she heard was just her imagination. Because this had been going on for some time—Louise calling, the guides responding, Louise blocking and calling again—there was an accumulation of energetic debris in her ear.

Louise needed to unclog the energetic stream (a personal ley line) so that she could hear what was occurring. We had her image the ear pain as a syrupy substance, then feel for it with her hand, get a hold of it, and gently pull it out of her ear.

She proceeded to do this, then frowned and stopped.

"There are too many voices speaking," she said. "I can't understand."

"Yes, this is often a problem at the start of such communication," I assured her. "There are many life forms who want to contact you, and now that they know you can hear them, everyone wants to present their information! They all are communicating at the same time, and it is simply too much for you to process! Focus again, and silently request your inner colleagues to please adjust their frequency, speak slower, and designate just one of them to speak at a time."

Louise went in to try again. When she returned to normal consciousness, tears began streaming down her face. "This is amazing," she said. "It is my guides who have been asking me to change my career! They say they want to help me!"

A frown suddenly crossed her face, and she spoke in a panic. "How will I talk to them when you're not here?"

"Don't worry," I said. "Once you have traveled the route yourself, you can find your way back."

We then began working out a process by which she could strengthen her connection to her team.

"The universe is very pragmatic," I explained to Louise. "When there is a need on all sides, it is easier to receive cooperation. Because you have already established with your guides a very grounded project you both want assistance with—changing your career—this will keep you working together and strengthen your bond. The success of the project will be the determining factor on how well you are able to meet the needs of one another.

"The next thing you need to do is to go back inside your heart and see a roundtable sitting there. This means that no one is higher or lower than anyone else. You and all your guides are equally important in determining the success of the project.

"You are going to put the topic to be discussed in the middle of this table. Everyone is free to express ideas, needs, and goals, and then come to a meeting of wills as to how to proceed. You are negotiating your team contract. These contracts are also renegotiable!

"See yourself sitting at the roundtable, with your hands resting on the table itself. This is so those coming to the table can see you are hiding nothing. You are to request them to do the same."

Louise closed her eyes to focus, eventually emerging to state that some of the guides had come to the table but others were hanging back in the darkness. Those she could identify included an angel, an owl, and her late grandmother; these were not forms she had ever consciously considered contacting.

"Go back in," I said, "and invite the guides who are hanging back to come forward and sit at the table as well. It is always the fairy godmother who is not invited to the party who causes the problems! You want to be sure all your guides are being well respected in this matter. Take your time, and really look at who is sitting at your table.

"Next, looking at the table as a clock with twelve positions, see where your guides are sitting. Once you can see who is sitting where, determine who is sitting at the cardinal directions and where you yourself are seated. Whoever is seated at the twelve o'clock position is the primary leader; it is usually a major energy form such as an angel. Where you are seated reflects your energy at this time; it could be at a cardinal point or some point in between. Next, see who is in the six o'clock position, then the three and nine o'clock positions. And then the points in between. Each of these positions has a different energy, and you need to understand what they are."

What I was explaining to her is similar to the positions on a Native American medicine wheel.

When Louise came back out, she told me she and her team were very much in agreement that they should start working, together, to plan a way for her to move from her corporate job into a gentler job where she could continue learning about energy. The first step was that by next week they would show her ways to reconfigure her current workspace so that it was more conducive to peaceful energy. Our session ended on this successful note.

Chapter 2

LESSONS

Each of us has an inner team. If you aren't aware of them, why not? Did you tell them to be silent, and since that was your free-will request to your own team, they complied? Did you never imagine they existed, thus when they did speak, you blocked the sounds or thought your imagination was simply very active that day?

Life on earth is very complex, and simply managing to incarnate in a physical body is a major achievement for a spark of infinite spirit! It can be daunting to master all the forces that seek to manifest in the physical realm, so spirit arranges for each of us to be backed up by many support team members.

Some of my clients come complaining about the dark forces who keep bothering them; they want my help to clear out the forces. I especially appreciate these sessions for I am always interested in what misunderstandings have occurred between humans and the energies of other worlds. Most of the time the energies they are complaining about are their guides who have come to assist because the person is calling on the universe for help. But because large segments of our society say that seeing and hearing subtle energies is bad or "sinful," the person has been scared by their appearance and is trying to send them away. The poor guides keep trying in every way possible to assist, and their human partners keep sabotaging them!

Sometimes there are dark forces bothering a person. Then I tell the client: "Look, you told your guides to stay away and not talk to you. Because this is a free-will universe, and they are of the light, they complied. That has left only the dark forces to speak with you, because they are not obligated to comply with your ordinary demands!

"Your best course of action is to tell your guides you apologize and please come back and help you. They will support your efforts to master your personal environment. Then, because it is a free-will universe, tell the dark energies very forcefully that they must leave you alone. Exerting your free will has two affects: it brings forth your own personal

84

willpower so that you can master whatever situation the dark force has come to teach you, and it turns aside those dark forces who have just come to make mischief for you."

This is a very good place to clarify any confusion that exists between what is called "channeling," "interworld" or "interdimensional communication," and "interdimensional cooperation," as I am using the terms in this book. These are three distinctly different processes.

In the past, "channeling" was sometimes used to refer to any contact with spirit in which a human is transmitting a message from spirit into our third dimension. In recent years, as the open knowledge of how to communicate between worlds has grown, new terms have come into being that describe different aspects of this overall situation.

Interworld contact can take place in many forms both positive and negative. This book focuses on teaching you how to be aware of what is occurring and how we are affecting each other when the worlds overlap. There are distinct differences in how you approach this process, and in the results produced by each approach. Your own intent is the primary motivating factor.

Interdimensional or interworld cooperation takes place between colleagues of different worlds. It is an active situation. It is based in the practitioner's spiritual awareness that there are many different worlds in this infinite span of universal consciousness and some of these occasionally energetically intersect with and affect each other.

Interdimensional or interworld communication refers to this process but includes a broader span of motivations. It could be positive and among equals. It could also be based in authoritarian energies, such as an occultist seeking to control and manipulate the energies of other worlds. This "power-over" approach has led to many of the current problems we have on earth; it is an energetic approach that has led to so many wars and leads to interworld wars as well. No one wants to be controlled by someone else, whether it is a nature spirit or a human being, and all life forms will eventually fight to regain their freedom. All life forms also have bigger brothers and sisters who will come to the rescue of their little brother or sister, when necessary, and occultism is a deep rabbit hole that is hard to climb out of.

Channeling, as defined by many energy workers today, is a more passive condition. It refers to the process by which a human gives over his or her free will to another life form who has stated he/she has a specific message to be transmitted, intact, to earth. The alien life form wants to use the human vehicle to deliver the message.

Throughout the ages, some sensitives have willingly become channels for the transmission of specific spiritual information that was essential for the evolution of the human state. This transmission can be conscious or unconscious.

"Unconscious" means the human either steps aside or is taken over by a stronger life-force energy who uses the human body to transmit a message to other humans. When the life form leaves the body, the human has no memory of what occurred during its "occupation." There is no learning or expansion of consciousness for the human in this case, and the process will gradually wear down the human's energy field, resulting in deteriorating health.

"Conscious" channeling means the human is receiving information from another world or dimension and is permitting the information to flow through, unimpeded. When the two energies are compatible, health is maintained and can even become stronger. My team's objection to this is that it keeps the human at an inferior level in the process. They feel the ultimate victory of the light depends upon humans growing in knowledge, to act as coequals with life forms of other worlds. They have insisted I learn to communicate with them, and they helped me expand my consciousness to do so.

Sometimes what our culture commonly refers to as channeling is actually communication. In ancient temple societies, specific individuals were taught how to leave ordinary consciousness to commune with the gods and bring back essential information for their people. This includes the oracle at Delphi, Greece, where, historians believe, the process involved the ingestion by a priestess of some sort of vapor at the site, which helped her break out of the third dimension to retrieve information from other dimensions. Some indigenous societies use herbs to break free of the bonds of the third dimension; this was sometimes necessary, especially during the Kali Yuga. Other societies will use drumming to free people from the bonds of the physical body so that they can move into frequencies where they can commune or speak with spirit.

Some people like to do what they call automatic writing, in which they go into a reverie and write down whatever flows through them. The results depend upon what energy the individual is choosing to allow to flow. This is an excellent way to permit subtle energies to descend into the physical level of consciousness, but the form the writings take depends upon how accurately the individual is able to translate the subtle energy flow into solid words. This can vary depending upon the consciousness of the individual at that time (have they been praying and meditating, or have they been arguing with someone else).

Eventually, to make any further progress in this process of communication with "spirit"—e.g., interdimensional communication—the break with the solid physical reality of our world is achieved; practitioners must assume conscious responsibility for their actions. They need to master expanding their normal consciousness so that they are consciously aware of these other worlds.

World consciousness has advanced to a state in which many humans can transition between worlds naturally, as part of their normal consciousness, without the need of herbs or vapors or automatic writing to help the process. This is what we are learning about in this book.

Many interworld communicators work on an individual basis, developing their own work and assisting others. Many great breakthroughs and "inventions" have occurred and countries have been saved—as with Joan of Arc and France—because some individual accurately "listened" to the voice of a guiding spirit and then used their personal free will to act on earth.

A number of secret and esoteric organizations have been founded based on the interactions between founders and their guides in other worlds.

Such is the case with Madame Blavatsky, one of the founders of the Theosophical Society.

A famous painting (see Figure 2.10) shows Madame Blavatsky surrounded by three of her most significant inner guides (left to right) Kuthumi, Morya and St. Germain. The painting shows that these guides are very real to her and could be drawn. (With today's photographic technology, they might even be photographed.) Madame Blavatsky credited these three guides, especially Kuthumi (also known as Master Koot Hoomi), as the source of much of her metaphysical knowledge and writings.

Figure 2.10. Madame Blavatsky with Kuthumi, Morya, and St. Germain.

Madam Blavatsky sometimes referred to her work, in the semantic style of the time, as telepathic communication. Later scholars, in the style of the 1900s, sometimes referred to her process of communication as channeling. Today, I consider her work to belong to the realm of interdimensional cooperation, because the clear conscious interaction between her and her guides demonstrates that they were working together for her to understand and transmit the fluid knowledge of spirit to the solid third-dimensional realm of humans.

The kind of cooperation that Madam Blavatsky experienced strengthens individuals, broadening their awareness and enabling them to perceive and act from a higher plane. It is based on a far different relationship between the worlds than what occurs in channeling.

True channeling, as I stated before, is a process that will often negatively affect the health of individuals. The human's body eventually experiences an auric weakening from the constant changes in internal frequency. An example of this is the presentation of the Seth material in the late 1960s. The channel Jane Roberts believed that stepping aside would permit the Seth material to reach earth, and she believed it important enough to sacrifice herself; she knew the transmissions weakened her, and eventually they led to her death.

Channeling an energy which is a part of you—such as your higher self or your soul family—need not weaken you, because the energies are compatible. A prime example of this is Ronna Herman, who channels Archangel Michael. She has stated that she is of Michael's family, hence working in this way actually strengthens her physical body and her inner connection to her soul group.

In some cases, dark forces want to channel through a person, and this type of situation serves as fodder for the tales of Stephen King and other horror story writers.

And in some cases life forms in other worlds keep contacting humans who then assume they are going mad because, I believe, they have not been objectively taught what is occurring. They may simply be in communication with life forms from other worlds who have bled into their awareness. We need to teach people how to understand, control, and work with these situations, not punish and abuse these sensitives! Some indigenous societies take these sensitive people and train them to be conduits to other worlds; all too often the West medicates them and puts them in hospitals!

By upgrading our abilities through conscious awareness and personal growth, we will create a stronger and more compassionate humanity. We the practitioners, along with our inner colleagues, are in charge of whatever situation we enter into.

Like the days when we had to learn that the world was not flat, we are moving into an awareness that the third dimension is not the only dimension that exists. We should get used to it and work with it! The explorers are the ones who break ground for all of us, and now this exploration is interdimensional.

Interdimensional or interworld cooperation is a steady, positive process in which human beings learn to extend their conscious awareness so that they can interact with life forms in other worlds. Solving issues in consultation with their inner teams strengthens people's ability to consciously work at will in different worlds.

Many recently born children—known as the Indigos, Crystals, and Rainbows—have come in with extended abilities to communicate with other life forms. If they are fortunate enough to have a receptive home environment, they maintain their original awareness as they mature. These young people are appearing around the world in the hundreds of thousands now and are representative of the new higher frequencies the earth is currently moving into.

The Blue Papaya youths—some as young as eight years old—can see energy that other people cannot, and during warm weather we visit local nature preserves where they experiment with nature spirit photography, with outstanding results. They learn from one another how to get into the proper energetic space to see and digitally record the energies they can see, hear, and/or feel. They then can specify where the life form is that they want to photograph, and that energy can be seen in the digital image.

They are communicating with life forms as equals; it is just another form of conversation for them.

I am a bit different from these children as I came to these abilities as a mature person; in the process of finding solutions to my health situation, I experienced unexpected contact with life forms from other worlds. The experience of going from unaware acceptance of my culture's belief that solid physical reality is the only one of value to an awareness that there are many other worlds and life forms affecting us has enabled me to explain how these types of perception interrelate. Today, my core team—the 3Ms: Archangels Metatron, Melchizedek, and Michael—are always present to teach me. They help many, many people, focusing on developing each individual's consciousness so that the human becomes an aware participant in earth's transformation. They help humans expand their consciousness according to their areas of interest and the level of their souls' evolution.

EXERCISE

Now that you know such communication is possible and real, let's put this knowledge into practice. We are going to start working with your inner team. Such practice solidifies your understanding.

The first step is to set your intent. The inner world is very big and very pragmatic; what you ask for is precisely where the energies will lead you. So you must be careful to specify what you want. For example, at the start you can address the universe in general: "Dear loving universe, please help me to gently and lovingly connect with my own inner team, and help me understand what is occurring when we connect."

Write down your intent. Study its wording carefully to make sure there are no hidden issues that will sabotage your results. For example, if you simply said "I want to connect right away to my guides," you might create a minor catastrophe; the universe might do something radical to get immediate results, such as having you experience a car accident that sends you out of body rapidly and into your guides' domains!

Next set aside a period of time—five minutes to half an hour—during which you will not be disturbed. For some people, this might take a bit of ingenuity; it might mean staying up late, getting up early, or going for a walk in the woods. You can always lie down quietly on your bed, look like you are asleep, and work through this exercise—although you do run the chance of really sliding into sleep!

Ideally, sit down quietly. State your intent.

Now we are going to take you through the process Louise experienced, only we are going to explain it in greater detail. Focus on your spiritual heart center, located in the center of the chest. Visualize, feel, sense, and/or hear—use whatever senses you depend upon most—a roundtable in the middle of your chest. Sit down at it and put your hands, folded, on top of the table. Focus your sight to sense the table form and where the clock-like cardinal directions are located—the twelve and six, then three and nine. Many people see the twelve as center front of their body, but this does not necessarily have to be so. Twelve o'clock is energetic north—the home of unmanifest spirit, the energies of winter when life is dormant. Six o'clock is energetic south—the home of full mature energy, the energies of summer when crops are fully grown. Three o'clock is the energetic east—the home of new life, the emerging seed, the energy of spring. Nine o'clock is the energetic west—the home of the harvest, the harvesting of the energy of the current cycle of seasons, the energy of autumn, and the preparation time for a return to spirit. The clock positions between these cardinal directions indicate a mix of the cardinal energies similar to the movement through the seasons in the temperate Northern Hemisphere climates. If you live in a different climate area, you will need to adapt the circle to the seasons in your area.

Next, locate the position at which you have chosen to sit; that determines the energetic position you consider yourself to be in at present. For instance, you might feel you are sitting at five o'clock, indicating you are just growing into your full "summer" energies.

Now call on your spirit guides, gently and with love, to please come forward and take their positions around the table, also with their hands folded on the table to signify they are open and not hiding anything. Watch quietly as they come forward from the mist of consciousness—you might see this mist as grey, white, black, blue, pink, etc. Some of your team will immediately come forward and sit. Others might hang back, perhaps because you have dismissed them so many times before they no longer feel welcome; if you sense this, apologize for not understanding and request they come forward to take their rightful places. There will still be some gaps—the absence of energies you have tried to send away because you did not understand their significance. Request they come forward and sit. Finally, request that any remaining beneficial energies who feel they belong at the table come forward; apologize for not recognizing them and request that they come forward now to take their rightful places.

Still sitting quietly, move your inner senses around the circle, and begin to discern who is sitting where. Let each position explain to you who they are; if this is not yet possible, don't worry, they will explain in time as you learn to see them more clearly. After you have checked in with your team to the best of your present awareness, acknowledge their presence and convene the meeting. In the center of the table place the matter you wish to discuss. It could be "how can we all work together consciously and harmoniously for the highest good of all?" Of course, if your team has an issue it really needs to discuss, it could request that be put in the center instead.

Next, quietly move sequentially about the roundtable, letting each team member express its viewpoint on the issue at the center. Finally, you as the moderator—the human component of the team—work with the group to come to a common consensus. This includes exactly what the core issue is, how to work through it, what the time frame is for working with the issue, by what criteria is "success" to be measured, and when you will next meet. Setting a measurement for success is important; it enables to you determine how successfully your team is working together, and it helps you develop faith in each other that you can do what you say you can do! Everyone then has their assignment, including you, and the meeting ends with all going off to do their part, to report back at the time agreed upon.

Keep practicing this exercise, and you will improve significantly in communicating with your team.

A few additional pointers:

Specify at the outset that you are going to work with the group as a part of a team. This means you have the right to argue with them about a course of action they may wish you to take. I sometimes do this, and the argument requires my inner team to clarify what they need accomplished and for me to explain the issues that come with manifesting this goal in the physical realm.

If your team wants you to work with them on a specific project, they may need to adjust some of their expectations of you. For example: inner guides don't need to sleep, eat, and pay the bills—these are third-dimension issues. So if they want you to help, they need to allow you time to relax, have fun, and they must work with you to develop a method by which you can generate income to pay your bills! This last item is a right many "spiritual" people have difficulty with!

If you would like more help with this situation, visit my website, crystal-life.com, where there are free downloadable exercises you can listen to and work along with.

PHOTOGRAPHS

Is it possible to photograph your guides? Perhaps you already are doing this and you don't even realize it! One of my spirit guides is Great Bear. He is very protective of me and images of bear will manifest in unusual places when I need confirmation that I am well protected in my work. When I accepted my guides' request to photograph, I began seeing bear images in nature scenes that particularly affected me. I have gone on photographic outings with people who have other totem animals—a hawk or wolf, for instance—and when they've pointed out these images to me, I've realized I hadn't seen them because I wasn't focused on that energy.

I often see bear spirit in the knots, burls, burrs, and roots of trees, for I am attracted to trees with that bear-like protective energy. Figure 2.11

is a friendly image of bear with two friends—a combined Redwood burl I came upon on a walk through a California redwood preserve.

Figure 2.11. Bear face in redwood burl.

When you are doing such photography, you need to keep your gaze soft and focused at the same time. Each tree has many faces, and if you are called to pause and observe a tree, walk about it slowly, looking up and down, and talk to the tree, asking it to show and share its secret form with you. Then request it let you photograph the form, to share respectfully with others. Emphasize you wish to help construct a cooperative world in which all forms love and honor one another. Take many photos, both up close and longer shots, all the while requesting the tree's cooperation. Ask it to stay still while you do your work; at the start of my work I would sometimes get clear shots until I reached the "sweet spot," and here the tree and I were both vibrating so strongly that the camera took a blurred shot. I learned to ask the spirit energy to hold still so I could get a good photo!

When you download the photos, request that your inner team and/or the tree spirit help you find the particular image, and place on the image, that conveys its energy. It is important to do this; often my camera will catch some energy on film that I didn't see with my physical eyes. Digital work on a computer is excellent for finding the important images, for you can zoom in and out. Shooting in a high pixel size enables you to blow up an image to see the spirit, which is sometimes very small!

Masonic Hauntings

Sometimes a practitioner cannot do anything to change a situation.

Melissa contacted me for a distance clearing on a home she had purchased against her husband's advice.

"This home is a defunct Masonic temple," she said. "My husband, Jim, did not want me to purchase it, but I insisted; it was a very good deal! Well, I soon discovered why! Right from the start—gutting the structure and rebuilding it as a home—we've had nothing but problems! There have been missing tools, dark specters lurking about, sounds heard where nothing can be seen.

"When we finally moved in, Jim and I began fighting about everything! There was no peace to be had between us, no matter how hard we tried!

We finally separated, and now I'm trying to sell the building to complete the divorce settlement. It's been on the market for two years, and no one has even made an offer!"

I discussed her situation with my inner team and reported back that there was nothing we could do. My team said Melissa needed to contact a Masonic group to perform a ceremony to clear the building of that order's protective energies, and only then would it sell.

Melissa indicated she did not really want to go that route and would look elsewhere for a solution.

Several years later, I met Melissa at a social function and asked what had happened with her home. "Oh," she replied, "I tried a number of solutions that didn't work. So I located a Masonic group who agreed to help. They came in and performed a closing ceremony. Shortly after that, the building sold."

Then she changed her tone. "I'm sooo glad to be out of that situation," she confided with obvious relief.

LESSONS

When a building has been used by a powerful ancient order with occult roots, such as the Masons, it comes with its own set of issues.

In this situation, the building had been properly opened, with ceremony, and ceremony had attended all the functions inside the building. This was good for its original purpose as it built up the energy of the life forms being worked with. It tied the building into the morphogenetic web of all Masonic temples everywhere.

However, in this case, the local order had slowly died out, and the building had been vacant for many decades. It was not a case in which an order had closed the building and performed a ceremony to end its occupation. The remaining Masons had intended to someday return, but with the death of the last of that local group, this had not occurred.

No closing ceremony had ever taken place, and the spirits of the order were still present. To them, an all-male order, not only was a stranger invading their secret society headquarters—it was a woman! The spirits were only doing their job, which was to protect the temple from those they considered had no right to be there, who they had been instructed to keep away. The new owners had not done a ceremony before starting to tear apart this small world, and this only served to further aggravate the guardians.

The Masonic order is a very ancient group. Even if a local chapter is not aware of such things as thought forms living at the site, they exist from the pervasive strength of the parent order throughout its own morphogenetic web. There are so many levels to a secret order such as the Masons that it is difficult for outsiders to work their way through all the energetic devices. As one energetic device is cleared, another comes forward.

The only solution is for a new owner to be certain that the order's clearing mechanism has been activated. The Masons know how to set up and dismantle their own temples. The same is true with other esoteric orders.

THE LADY WHO LIVED IN THE DARK

Ida had remarried about four years ago, and she and her new husband had bought a home in a new housing development. It was situated on a several-acre parcel of what had been an old farmstead.

Since moving in, Ida's health had deteriorated significantly to a point where she could not stand sunlight and kept shades in her house pulled down. She also could not stand to be near electronic equipment. Unfortunately, her husband was a computer consultant and had a lot of electronics in the house.

Ida said she had an additional problem: she saw movements in the living room as she walked by and was worried that there were evil spirits trying to harm her. So with all this going on, she called me to come check it out.

I arrived on a sunny day and, before entering the home, surveyed the surrounding area, checking out the energies and potential problem spots. It was a bucolic scene: the wide-open prairie filled with blossoming pink milkweed, a low limestone farm wall meandering through the prairie and leading, in the distance, to a small wooded hillock. The land parcels were large, the nearest neighbor a quarter mile away.

Ida was waiting when I knocked at the front door. She announced from the other side, "I'm going to unlock the door, but wait before you come in! I'll go into the kitchen so the sunlight doesn't hurt my eyes!" I waited a few moments as I heard her walk away, then entered. As I walked into her kitchen, I passed the living room on the right and was aware of spirits watching me. Clearly Ida had some house issues!

Ida was a sturdily built woman with the dry, slightly nervous, upper solar plexus energy that signals potential electromagnetic problems—that includes sensitivity to the electromagnetic frequencies of computers, electronics, and spirits.

After listening to her interpretation of the situation, it was time to examine and talk with the house itself. I walked through the rooms, checking out the energy fluctuations, and ascertained that her husband did indeed have a large number of computers running for his business but that he was not affected. He had the oilier Mediterranean–Near Eastern complexion and the heartier, lower solar plexus energy that is not as affected by third-dimension electromagnetic frequencies.

In the kind of partnering that often occurs in marriage, these two people were opposite in their sensitivity to electricity, and it was clear the husband, while sympathetic, had no understanding at all of what was occurring to his wife.

Yes, the energy was strong around his machines, but they had already adjusted their living space for Ida's sensitivity by moving his home office to one end of the house, away from her living areas. It became clear that Ida had been put in the presence of so many electromagnetic issues for so long that her own energy field could no longer process them and was breaking down. So, for me, it became a matter of mapping out how, what, and where the energies were. One strong source was the electromagnetic energy of the spirits, which were focused in the living room.

I went into the living room and sat on one of the two couches that faced each other on either side of a glass coffee table, and I waited. Slowly a group of Native American spirits dressed in buckskins emerged to my inner sight. They were sitting on the couch opposite mine, staring at me solemnly and silently. When they finally chose to communicate, it was a short, simple statement, made without emotion but with determination. "You are sitting in our space," they said. "So is the house. We want you out and our land returned to us."

I sat silently and observed. Between us, where the coffee table now rested, a vortex emerged; it should have functioned as a negative counter-spinning energy that helped pull in and send off negative, dead energies, but its energy had been cut off during the housing development's construction. Then the image took the form of what the area had once been—a long-ago abandoned Native burial site. These spirits had been living on the site; some were the original thought forms put in place to protect it, and others were humans buried there who had chosen to join the thought forms as guardians of place.

When the Western builder leveled the land, perhaps unaware of its long-ago use, the graveyard ceased to be. But, as in the "Guardian of the Spring" story, these spirits still remained on the site, now without a function or an area of their own in which to congregate. They wanted their function back, their site back, and the interlopers gone. The end. No discussion.

I stood up, went to the window at the far end of the living room, and looked out. The house next door stood on a portion of a positive vortex that had been linked to the negative one in this home. The two vortexes had once been paired and together had helped keep the area clear. The energy around the other home indicated its owners would not be receptive to subtle land adjusting, which Ida later confirmed. Therefore, it would not be possible to reactivate and connect the two vortexes, both of which were now blocked.

Here was the crux of Ida's health issues: unable to feed off the negative vortex, the spirits were pulling on her energy. It was not malicious in intent. They needed food to survive, and she was there. They were no more enthusiastic about the situation than she was.

I called Ida into the room and had her take my place on the sofa while I moved to an armchair outside the circle of energy. My team and I set space and held it, bringing the frequencies of the spirits and Ida into alignment with each other so that they could hear, see, and communicate— much to Ida's surprise. I say "surprise," but actually humans are always very comfortable communing with spirits once we are underway. That is because, once underway, humans often admit they have been aware of the life forms but thought it was only their imagination. The situation is actually a normal occurrence—or one that should be normal if humans only remembered that conscious life exists on many more levels than just the third dimension of solid form.

Negotiations began.

Our small negotiating group of humans and spirits established that it was not an option to destroy the house and return the land to nature. That time was gone, as were many of the energies the spirits had once felt at home with. We established the fact that they did not want to transition to the light, as they felt they were guardians of the land and that was their free-will choice. They wanted a home to call their own, undisturbed by these modern people, where they could continue their protection of this area. They did not know what to do now or where to go, and they wanted help.

"Ida," I said, "do you know of any place nearby whose energy is comparable with this land, where the spirits could live and not be disturbed?"

She thought for a few moments, then smiled. "There's a clearing on the hillock that I've always enjoyed because of its peaceful energy. The hill is part of a nature preserve, so it won't be built up."

We presented this option to the small group of spirits. They said they were willing to go, but they did not know how to get there and were afraid to leave their current space. This is a common situation with some spirits and guardians of place, as well as with simpler nature sprites, who are site specific. It's like a circle of frequency is drawn around them, defining their spirit property, and they don't step outside their safe domain. Some people are like that, too!

In cases such as this, sometimes a human who can see the spirits, or nature sprites, will serve as a tour guide, leading the spirits to the new territory.

So we asked the spirits: "Will you go if Ida holds out her hand, and one of you is connected to her, and so on down the line, so that you are all connected to one another?" They agreed this would work for them.

Now it was Ida's turn to balk. She was fine with serving as guide for the spirits, but she no longer went outside except at dusk and dawn because she could not endure the sun! So it was negotiated that the walk would occur at dusk the following evening. Ida would lead the group across the several fields between the hillock and her house, about a mile in all, and take the group to the new site. With negotiations in place and set in spirit agreement, the session was over.

Ida called a week later to report: she had led the spirits to the site, as promised, feeling them physically holding onto her hand. When they reached the site, the spirits had released her hand and settled in. She felt responsible for them, however, and the next three nights, from her home, she had inwardly checked in with the small group of spirits to be certain they were happy.

On the third night, the spirits told her they liked the site. "You should leave us alone now," they exclaimed, "and don't come back!"

Ida also reported, with great relief, that she had now opened the curtains in her home, except at midday, and was excited about her recovery.

Lessons

Very often dimensions intersect, as they did at Ida's house. These intersections occur at vortex points, where some of the many lines of energy that grid all worlds in the universe happen to cross or are consciously made to cross. The forces at these cross locations naturally generate a spiral of energy—a vortex, spiral, or tunnel—which serves as a portal, gateway, or passage between energy sectors. When a spiral passes through several layers of grids, the portal is more significant for it can take us a farther distance through time/space. It is sometimes useful to utilize these portals for travel. At other times it may be necessary to close the portal to prevent such travel from occurring, or to shift it to another location.

Where the previous use of a piece of land has involved intense energies—for example, at a battlefield, ceremonial site, or burial site such as at Ida's—emotional and mental earth energies, as well as energies of other realms, have been consciously or unconsciously invoked. There have been intense calls that moved through the energy fields as they sought a path for an answer, and these created "tunnels" or "cords" through layers of grids. The emotions and the energies of this situation are held in place by these cords and become a part of the permanent energies of that piece of land. The shape looks and acts like an anchor: a vertical line up and a horizontal line spreading out at a specific location.

Energy travels along lines of light, just as our third-dimension electricity travels along physical cords. Energy has more options for travel, however, including going through time/space fields—such as between earth and some far point of the galaxy (a "wormhole")—or between some past incident that was so intense it either imprinted itself on a location and expanded out into other times/spaces or was projected into another time/space location.

Life forms and energies that coexist with us are not necessarily bad or evil, or good and benign. They are manifestations of consciousness, just as we are, and they have their own range of abilities, needs, and wants. At Ida's, the energies were consciously aware and chose to remain present to perform their tasks even though the physical use of the land had changed. In the original creation of the grave site thought forms, the prime directive had been to protect and maintain, and as other life forms joined the primary group, they took up this directive as well. They had received no input that the situation had changed and were simple enough forms that they could not conceive of adjusting to the new situation until we helped them do so by consciously communicating with them.

In this way they are much like humans who cannot conceive of there being a cause of their problem occurring in another dimension, until someone explains how this can occur. An early teacher of mine, BioGeometry's Dr. Ibrahim Karim,[10] is fond of stating that if a concept is not in a person's database, they are unable to see it even when it is right in front of them.

It is always better to avoid the kind of conflict that occurred at Ida's over the use of a particular piece of land. When you know of a site where construction is going to occur, take the initiative. Go there ahead of time, and alert the energies of that area so that they can help the local spirits relocate. Even if you think they are your imagination, or that they cannot hear you, they can, especially if you focus with intensity and the honorable intent to assist them.

A friend—a big, gentle bruiser of a guy—goes to natural sites about to be bulldozed for construction. He contacts the faery people—the simple ones who are committed to the plants and energies of the site and who die when such destruction occurs because they don't know what to do. He talks with them and then gets into his car, gently holds out one of his massively large fingers for the little faeries to hold onto, and slowly drives the giggling line of happy little ones to a safe new location! We did something similar here: we had Ida lead the spirits to a new location.

The "old ways" of calling in a person of spirit to ascertain that a specific location would be appropriate to build on and to ask for a land clearing and blessing was a practical method of procedure to avoid the kind of situation that occurred with Ida. Unfortunately we have become too "civilized" to do this, which causes considerable problems for people who then unwittingly move onto that site.

EXERCISE

In the previous stories, you've learned how guardians and spirits of place can affect your home. Let's work with locating the beneficial spirit of place in your home.

Find a quiet time when you will not be disturbed. Think about your home and the point you consider its energetic center—it could be the living room, family room, kitchen, or elsewhere. Go to that point, place a chair there, and sit down. Center yourself—here is a basic way to do this:

Sit with your spine straight, both feet on the floor, hands relaxed and perhaps folded on your lap, or one on each knee. There is a central channel of energy running through the human body; if you hold your thumb and forefinger together in a circle, its core is about this diameter. This channel is called different names by different traditions, the members of whom may also be focusing on various substrata of this energy. Such names include the central channel, the sushumna, and the haric line.

The central channel runs all the way from source/spirit down through the body and into the core of the earth or of the universe. Most traditions see this as a transition from spirit to matter, male vision to female creation; you exist as a manifestation on the earth plane of this one continuous energy. This flow is actually circular in motion, going continuously from spirit to matter, then making a thin loop back up to rejoin spirit from whence it circles back down again. Watch the energy flow. Then focus on the spiritual heart center in the center of your chest and in the center of the column of energy; inside this is where your personal journey has begun—your soul seat. Give out a puff of air—expanding this point of light in your soul seat to surround your energy field; it is about three feet in horizontal diameter. Call your inner team to be with you while you explore. This is a good way to start every exploratory session!

Next, gently and kindly call on the spirit of place to please come forward and visit with you. This spirit is the energy who is in charge of your home or of this room. Ideally, the spirit is happy, active, respected, and working to keep your home clear and energized. However, there may be problems, and these you want to know about. Request that the spirit tell you how it is doing and if there is anything you can do to further optimize your home's energy. Listen to its concerns, and ask in what way you can assist. Then do what you're told—make the change, or discuss why you cannot. And continue your dialogue at a future time!

Very often the spirit of place resides in a specific location—a sweet spot that you can feel, a place where you especially like to sit or walk through. There is also a spirit of place for each room. This spirit's job is to see that the energy of that room is the best it can be. Parents can locate that point in a child's room and stand there. The spirit can, if it wishes, express to the parent what the child is actually going through right then, and say how the parent can support the child's inner development; this is profoundly useful, especially with teenagers, who can be very silent about issues that are troubling them.

However, I've also cleared homes where, the instant I call on spirit of place, the form comes forward and roundly complains about the owner who is doing something harmful, totally unaware of how it is affecting the spirit. In one instance, the owner had placed a discordant statue half on the sweet spot, which was badly distorting the spirit's energy. In another instance, the spirit came forth and said how much it appreciated the owner who took such good care of the home!

The Horse Who Knew More Than His Owners

Several years ago, the McGrearys purchased, for a very good price, a large parcel of prairie that had once been a working farm. They were now having severe health issues, and because nothing else had worked, they called me in to assess their land and personal health.

My heart sank as I drove up to their house one warm and sunny summer day. The beautiful piece of land stretched way back from a main road, with their house in the middle, a horse stable in the back, and strung out cattycorner across the back of the property, crossing within the corral area, was a very tall, very wide line of "marching" power lines. I could see and sense the energy leaking and looping out from those monsters!

To add to the unfortunate situation, the energy of the area was dry, which is a powerful EMF (electromagnetic field) conductor, and there were very few trees to counteract the EMFs; trees such as evergreens are very good at siphoning off electronic pollution. The large tower nearest the stable and the McGreary home had been unwittingly placed on a major ley line that traveled crosswise down the entire length of the family property, passing some fifty feet from the home. Most of the plant life along that ley line was yellow, stunted, or seriously warped.

The whole McGreary family gathered in the living room and explained the situation as they understood it. They all showed the effects of severe electromagnetic pollution. Their energy was dull and their skin soggy—a "look" that occurs as electromagnetic pollution is absorbed into the body. Everyone in the family was having digestive problems, diarrhea, and skin issues. Their nerves were seriously jangled. Moreover, the wife had an asymmetrical face; the left side was smaller than the right and had less energy flowing through it. This is usually a sign that there is an electrical issue involved, because most people pull in energy on the left side and send out energy from the right side. General electricity pulses at the human energy field level and is a short frequency range compared to that of nature. When the body cannot pull in its electrical food from nature, it begins to shrink.

The family members were concerned about their own health and the health of their horses. There were currently two horses in residence. One, a long-time resident whose health was stable, was standing in a corner farthest from that tower. This was his favorite spot. The other, recently purchased and whose health was deteriorating, was drinking from a water trough the family had unknowingly placed right on the polluted ley line. We watched as that horse repeatedly nudged the trough with his nose.

"The horse has been giving us such problems," Mr. McGreary complained. "He keeps nudging the trough until it's ten feet away from where we place it; we have to keep going out and repositioning it." The horse clearly sensed the energetics of the situation far better than the humans did!

The McCrearys were puzzled by that horse's poor health. "We buy a healthy horse, then its health starts to deteriorate. Then, when we sell it, it regains its health with its new owner."

The "funny" thing about power lines is that their energy loops out. If an object is in the weak part of this wave, the energy is bearable. If an object is on the loop itself, the object feels it strongly. And if an electrical source is not properly grounded and the wires not properly insulated, the energy can go into the ground itself and pulse out so that animals placed there will sometimes shift their feet in rhythm to the electric oscillation, in an attempt to alleviate the situation. Lifting one foot keeps the electrical current from grounding through their body, hence the restless look of such animals. Animals forced to live in such an area begin to lose their vibrant energy, and their coats get dull and mangy. The horse who had lived there a long time had found a safe area where the loop was not touching down; the newer horse had not.

I showed the McGrearys these various situations and explained that the energy was so strong, the best option was for them to move. Avoidance of such a powerful issue is always the best option. However, as so often happens in cases such as this, the family was not interested in moving away. They said they had been able to afford this land, which had been sold at a lower rate than surrounding horse farms, and they would not be able to replicate such a "deal" elsewhere!

Surrendering to what was by now, unfortunately, a frequent story, I began searching for other options that could at least assist the family in regaining their health. The first step was to contact the power lines themselves; they were not interested in negotiating. Their attitude reminded me of some bully nations or humans in situations in which they are clearly the dominant force and don't need to negotiate for their own sakes.

The best that could be achieved in this situation was to help the family mitigate the effect of the major ley lines. They needed to make certain they did not place along either line any objects with which they needed to be in repeated or prolonged contact—especially along the one the power lines were on and the one crossing that. They also needed to move the water trough out of the electrical loop so that the horses could drink healthier water. Water conducts electrical energy, so when electrical current goes through water on a ley line, the problem is amplified. The third strategy was to see if there was some way to shift the affected horse's stable stall (which was clearly affected, while the other horse's stable stall was not), and extend the corral in the area farthest from the tower where the other horse hung out. That horse had commandeered the small clear space for himself, not letting the newer horse use it—a sensible self-protection for the alpha horse.

The house was on another loop of the power line, so the solution was to install a mitigating device—a Slim Spurling agricultural harmonizer, which is a merkabah shape developed by a team of people, some of whom had been teaching at the Colorado School of Mines. The harmonizer is a geometrically measured globe of gold-plated copper wire whose shape makes it emit a bubble of clear energy that spans a several-mile radius. The energy of this harmonizer can be amplified further by placing a set of headphones over it and playing into its structure an environmental CD that consists of different types of water frequencies. The rotating frequencies clear different levels of the water in the atmosphere, thus strengthening the overall health of the area. It would have enough strength, when running with the CD, to help keep the farm energy clear.

I also recommended that each of the humans wear an EMF ceramic clearing pendant and that they plait a ceramic clearing bead into the horses' manes. These ceramic devices are based on ancient Egyptian/Atlantean faience and resonantly help to rebalance the energy fields back to zero point optimal health. Of course, everything has its limits, and clearing devices can only mitigate in the case of steady unhealthy oscillations such as what this family was enduring.

This was all I could do to assist the family.

LESSONS

It is a funny thing about humans in situations like this. Many times even when the family knows their health is being affected, they place financial considerations first. In one sad situation in which a family had one of the large marching power lines near their backyard, everyone in the family was affected with cancer of some sort and they were dying, one after another. The grandmother, Annette, who owned an aura-reading business, knew this and told them to move, but they would not because, they said, medical bills were so high, they could not afford a move. The lack of logic astounds me.

In another situation, when I was taking a lapidary workshop on Long Island, Jim, one of my classmates, was speaking about a local benefit a community was holding to help pay the cancer treatment bills for his nine-year-old grandson, Jimmie, who had leukemia. Something was not ringing right about the story. I questioned Jim, who eventually explained that his grandson would sit on the local generator station, which was in the family's front yard, while he waited for the school bus each morning. I told him to have the family stop the child from doing this; he looked at me like I was crazy.

Jim and I saw each other a few years later, and I asked after his grandson. By this time the knowledge of the effect of electrical fields was more widespread. Jim reported that not only had the family moved away from that house and the generator, but there had also been a study done at Jimmie's school. It turned out that the teachers on one side of the building, where a large cell-phone tower was, had a far higher incidence of cancer and leukemia than teachers on the other side of the building. For several years, Jimmie had been in classes on the side closer to the tower. Unfortunately, in spite their best efforts, Jimmie was not doing well at this time and was not expected to live much longer.

Sometimes when a family learns about the problems with their property, they feel a moral obligation not to sell to someone else. In some cases, that is honorable, and it is quite a financial dilemma. In other cases, I can see that a current owner has the genetic predisposition for EMF sensitivity (dry skin, a nervous disposition) whereas the previous owner did not (darker Mediterranean skin with an oilier base, operating more from the lower part of the solar plexus). In a case such as this, it would depend upon who bought the house. I tell the owners that as long as they are careful about this, and ask assurance from the house deva that it will work out, they can be at ease about the sale. If a house is in close proximity to one of the community generators that are way stations for underground electricity, it helps to plant evergreen bushes such as yews all around the generator, place large boulders that can mitigate EMFs such as granite and obsidian, and make certain children do not play near it. Also, an assessment of any looping effects from the generator should be made, and alleviating measures should be taken at those spots.

EXERCISE

Look around your house for power lines and step-down transformers. Are there generators for underground lines near your property? If you locate any, start observing how the energy of that device loops out. Sometimes you are safe because you are inside the loop, or the loop stops before the house. But other times the loop might cut across an important area of your home, necessitating your moving a bed or sofa. If you have in-ground generator stations, consider what types of bushes you could plant around them and at what distance, in keeping with local ordinances. Evergreens such as yews and pines are good buffers, absorbing the frequencies and actually thriving on this energy. Learning to feel/sense the path of these energies helps you create a healthy environment.

THE JILTED HOUSE—SPIRIT OF PLACE

Ralph and Mildred were having trouble selling their home and called me in to assess the situation. Here is what happened, in the husband's own words:

> Atala, we are so grateful for the time we spent together and for the phenomenal job you did in assisting me in dealing with my house and the transition. As you know, the house sold the next day after your visit with us. Thank you again for sharing your insight, abilities, and spirit with us.

I want to thank you most sincerely for your visit to our home two days ago. As you know, we have been trying to sell our home for several months with increasingly frustrating results. We had faced myriad physical problems with the house and two failed offers from buyers who were insincere and unqualified. We had become a bit disheartened and anxious especially since we had already purchased the new home and were facing an unacceptable financial drain owning one home too many. We had tried everything we knew, and some that folks told us about, to help the house sell faster, like baking cookies, placing candles and flowers around the home, burying a St. Joseph statue in the yard, etc. Nothing seemed to work, and our level of concern had increased a lot.

My wife had heard about your special abilities, and we decided to meet you in spite of some admitted reservations. You put us all at ease immediately, explained the theories of your work, and began a process which opened our eyes to a new realm of communication and connection we never even thought existed. I was brought to a place where I could connect with my house in incredible ways and reach wondrous insights into myself and my relationship with the world around me. It was an amazing evening filled with joy and tears and wonder. I felt a sense of peace I had lacked for months. All was in order, and things seemed calm and tranquil.

One day later, a perfect buyer fell in love with the home, made a significant offer which we were thrilled to accept following only a short negotiation, and the closing date was set for six weeks forward. I do not believe in accidents or coincidences. By any definition, something wonderful happened that evening, and the result was a perfect solution to the entire situation. Now, I, my wife, my family, and my home are most appreciative of your skillful and effective assistance. Thanks to you, all the spirits are happy and can move on to new lives and new experiences. We all thank you so very much.

Lessons

Sometimes people ask me to assess why a house is not selling. The house may have been on the market for months, at a very reasonable price, and it may even have had buyers who were interested who then backed away.

To solve this issue, I go into the home and determine with its owners exactly what they feel the problem to be or what they need to have resolved. Then I go for a walk by myself throughout the home and property and listen to the complaints and problems and aspirations of the beings connected to the issue at hand. This includes the house spirit, the resident devas, nature spirits, and any other life forms from other dimensions who feel they have a say in the matter.

Each home has a resident spirit who supervises that energy field. The spirit's domain is everything concerned with the house and its goings-on, including the well-being of the residents of the house. You can learn to talk to a home, and it will respond if you are kind to it and gentle.

Above local time and space, many life forms exist simultaneously in the same field. It is only the energetic agreement of the life forms involved in a situation that determines what time, space, and place is commonly perceived.[11] So in this situation I am only looking for the issues related to the specific topic at hand: the blockages to the sale of the home. I am not interested in occurrences in any other frequency line.

Very often, I will find the house spirit bitter, frightened, or afraid. It has done its utmost to protect and nourish the resident family, and now they are simply leaving it, turning it over to who knows what kind of family. They are doing so without even discussing or notifying the house of the reason for the sale, without a thank you or an expressed desire to find a buyer who will be kind to the home. There are frequently several key points around the property that are holding the distressed energy, and these points need to be adjusted, to shift. I listen, adjust my perceptions with all this new information, and then return to the home to discuss the matter with the family.

Let's face it. If I tell a normal American family their home is unhappy because it is not being consulted about its sale, they will think, at best, that I have a very active imagination. And nothing will be resolved for anyone.

So instead, as I mentioned in the introduction, I create a safe space for all the parties involved and bring the family and the home into discussion with each other.

It doesn't seem to matter whether the humans believe or not. The house selects the person it relates to most thoroughly and communicates with this individual. I've seen grown men—including executives who were reluctant participants only at their wives' wishes—burst into tears as the house speaks to them and expresses its anguish at the way it is being treated. When one person in the family can hear and feel the home talk to him or her—and recognize the feeling as being authentic—then all parties are more likely to resolve the distressing situation and create a positive outcome. Invariably, after everyone discusses the situation and clears the air, the house sells quickly. The obstacle to the sale, coming from the house itself, has been removed.

EXERCISE

Learn to communicate and cooperate with the deva of your living space! Sit quietly in a central area of the house. Call in your team, and request the house deva to make itself known—or ask your team to contact the house deva and ask it to communicate. Sit silently and scan for a response in some way—sense, feel, hear, see. Whether you do or do not consciously connect, thank the deva for protecting you and your family and the house itself. Ask the deva if there is something he/she feels is needed that you have not provided, and if the deva tells you something, discuss whether it is possible to provide this and whether you need the deva's assistance to do so.

There is also a deva for each room in a house. Over time, go to each room and locate the "sweet spot"—the point where the deva resides. Repeat the exercise above, and work with the deva to optimize the energy of that room.

In the course of my consultations, there have been a variety of responses when I have done this on behalf of the client. In one case, the room deva came forward instantly and asked me to have the owners remove that horrible statue they had placed half on the sweet spot, thus disabling the energy for that room. In another case, the room deva told me to have the mother of the teenage boy living in the room come stand inside the sweet spot. She told the mother that if the mother would come and stand there, she could become aware of the emotional issues the teenage son was experiencing and not sharing; the deva wanted the mother to know so she could assist the son. In yet another case in which a house was not selling, the house deva told the owner that she wanted only a family with young girls because the current family's girls had grown up and moved out, and the deva missed that energy; the owner then focused successfully with her real estate agent on locating such a family, who bought the home right away!

Whatever your personal story or issue, enlisting the help of the house and room devas is a smart energetic way to proceed!

• 3 •

Earth Energies

Time Travel

There was a mature grove of magnolia trees on the Swarthmore College campus where I went to school. The grove housed several time/space portals well known to energy workers of that area, but unfortunately, since the time of this story, it has been paved over to serve as a parking facility for a new dormitory. This is a shame because the energy was especially clearing and useful for the students, and I unconsciously used it often when I was there.

This grove was full of beautiful old Southern magnolia trees with wonderful gnarly trunks that curved gently, with many Y-splits just the right height for a teenager to sit in and get drunk on spring magnolia flower scent. I enjoyed sitting in the magnolia trees when I was a student. The college was very demanding in its academic requirements, and I needed the grove's nourishing, clarifying, and expansive energies.

Many decades later I was chatting with some customers at a Body-Mind-Spirit Expo when they told me about some famous interdimensional portals at a Pennsylvania college. "We're taking an overnight trip just to experience it," they exclaimed.

Curious, I asked which college. "Swarthmore," they replied. They went on to explain that magnolia tree energy is especially compatible with interdimensional travel.

So, of course, on my next alumni visit to campus, I had to investigate the situation. First I explored the dynamics of the grove itself. It existed within two distinctly different environments inside a single circle of energy. Half of this circle had verdant green grass and clockwise, dynamic, yang energy. The other half had very little grass growing—it was primarily dirt—and the energies were counterclockwise and yin. Here were two aspects of an energy field existing together within a common field—like a classic yin/yang circle. The energy of the whole was healthy, strong, and open; there was no stacking of negative energies around the area's perimeter, as is found when only one polarity is prevalent in a vortex. While the circles were strong and evident, they were integrated with their environment. "Well, this is nice," I concluded, all out of ideas for further exploration.

An amused voice responded to my thoughts. "Would you like to know how the portals work?" the grove's deva teased.

She was gentle, and her energy felt familiar—perhaps we had been in unconscious contact when I was a student there. So I was not even surprised that I could hear her, and I asked her to teach me.

The lesson began and continued for almost an hour. The deva had me walk from one side of the circle to the other to sense the different energies. She then had me visit many of the trees to sense their individual energies. She led me to a magnolia tree standing by itself in the yin circle of energy. It had a low Y-split, and she had me stand behind the left side trunk and line up my sight to another magnolia tree with a low Y-shaped trunk branching, located in the middle area between the two fields. I was instructed to focus through that Y to a third magnolia tree that was growing in the verdant yang area and that had curved branches overlapping to form a vesica pisces—an oval opening that occurs when two lines curve over each other (there is an implied intersecting of two circles in this form). (See Figures 3.1 and 3.2)

Figure 3.1. The magnolia portal. Note the base tree at the front right (and the nature spirit who was instructing smiling at us), the Y-sighting tree in the middle, and the two branches of the magnolia at the rear forming a vesica pisces. The photo was shot from the grassy yang side; the vesica pisces in use is in the yin side; notice the dirt area beginning.

Figure 3.2. This is a view back through the trees from the other side of the photo above. The dirt area is in front, and the grassy area in back. Note the magnificent vesica pisces formed by magnolia tree branches, the Y-tree in the middle, and the left branch anchoring site seen through that. Also note how clear and straight the land lines are.

After ascertaining, with some amusement, that I had no idea the significance of all this, the deva explained:

"There are three essential parts to this type of a portal. The first element is a base location, the time/space frame from which you start and to which you wish to return. This base location can be either a loved one whose frequency you are very familiar with or a specific distinctive object—in this case, the tall straight magnolia tree.

"The second element is a stabilizing object." She directed my attention to the Y-shaped tree. "You need to line up your energy to sling it into another dimension," she explained. "For this, a Y-shaped tree is always very useful." The first image I inwardly saw was my brother Chet as a child, playing with his slingshot. The next was remembering something I had learned: pagans find forked trees to be especially powerful for nature work.

"The third element, and the most important, is the oval vesica pisces through which the energy moves into another dimension. That is usually formed by two branches of a tree gently curving over each other. Very often, as in this case, the energy seen inside the portal is shimmering and of a different quality than what is outside."

When the deva said this, I immediately saw my BioGeometry® instructor, Dr. Robert Gilbert, who just the previous summer had taught me that a vesica pisces implies two circles of energy that cross over each other, creating an opening, or doorway, into other dimensions. He explained the Masons understand this concept very well and in medieval churches would draw or sculpt Jesus and the saints inside or emerging from a vesica pisces. This subconsciously energetically conveyed to the observer the image of new energy emerging on earth. Here the vesica pisces formed of magnolia branches was also creating an energetic doorway into other dimensions or cosmic locations.

As always when I receive instruction from nature spirits, as soon as I learn what is occurring, it becomes simple, clear, logical, and effective. "Of course," I said inwardly to the deva. "Now why didn't I see that before?!"

The deva laughed. "So," she said, "that is what is needed to travel out. Now how do you get back?"

I stood there, silently puzzled by this concept. I hadn't thought about that!

"You are traveling to another time/space location," the deva explained. "When you are ready to come back, how do you know where and when to stop? You could keep going into another time/space location."

This was clearly becoming more complicated and potentially dangerous than I had expected—not an uncommon occurrence for me when I learn from nature beings. The situation is much the same in our physical world. The principle is simple, and the complications occur when the principle is placed into action! I felt a bit wary and very alert. The deva sensed this and seemed pleased. She suggested I walk to the other side of this interdimensional gate and sight back.

"The problem on return," she stated, "is ending up in the same place from which you started. Otherwise, you can feel out of sorts: not quite 'back in your body,' or in another time/space location altogether.

"When you're working with this type of a situation," she continued, "it is wise to go with at least one other person whose frequency you know well enough to connect to on return; that will help you find the correct time/space location. The other option is to identify with an object in the space. In this situation, the energies can sight through the vesica pisces, through the Y, and hit the tree."

The deva had me walk back to the tree and sight again. "Well," she said, "what would happen if energies repeatedly slingshot through the energy portal, through the Y in the middle tree, and hit the stabilizing tree to stop?"

"I have no idea," I replied.

"Don't you think it would flatten the bark of the tree at that spot?" she suggested. "Go around the tree and look."

Sure enough, the bark on the front of the tree, exactly at the sighting spot, was extremely flat, unlike the bark on the other parts of the trunk.

"Do you want to try this for yourself?" the deva asked.

I considered her question. I had no intent or purpose at this moment other than understanding the principles; there was nowhere else in time/space that I wanted to go; so I declined.

It seemed to please her very much that I was not being greedy or rash. I felt a peaceful grid of understanding descend into my energy field as she gifted me with the new and greater appreciation for the untapped opportunities available to humans when we work in harmony with nature.

We thanked each other for the lovely interlude, and I went on my way.

Lessons

You've seen the problems people have when buildings have been built over energetically rich or troubled earth spots. The world loses when humans ignorantly destroy our earth heritage. Here in a magnolia grove was a time/space portal, managed by a very intelligent and kind deva; it had been of energetic use to generations of people, on many levels. Instead of working with the situation, and around it, years after the time of this story and photographs, the grove was paved over to create a parking lot; human will was wantonly imposed on nature, simply because people felt that humans *owned* the land. They never even considered the possibility of *developing* or *using* that specific spot of land in *cooperation* with the life forms of other realms who occupied it.

It is a shame when events such as this occur, for it weakens the energy of the area for all the life forms involved.

EXERCISE & PHOTOGRAPHS

A colleague called me in tears. The owner of the property across the street from her had brought in a tree company and they were in the process of cutting down a whole line of ancient, old growth oak trees. She had asked them to stop and had called the police, but the owner was a political big shot and no one would listen to her. She could feel the pain of the trees and the sorrow of the nature spirits in the entire area.

I told her that because she had done all she could, she should now sit silently and pray and meditate with the trees. She could at least alert the nature spirits to the extent of the impending devastation so that they could get their people out safely. She could send love to the trees being cut down so that they could peacefully transition to spirit.

She did this, then went on to work with her local community to put in place ordinances protecting old growth trees. Now no one can cut down a large old growth tree without permission from the township, and if such event is underway, a call will immediately bring the police.

I have heard ghastly tales of ancient trees being cut down for profit and concerned citizens unable to stop the massacre. These trees may be essential to the health of the local energy grid, and wantonly destroying them can create a cascade of unpleasant results from land issues to human health problems. The trees should be honored for their work, not callously destroyed.

What are the ordinances in your area for the protection of our natural environment? Do you care to make a difference? This exercise requests that you research your local ordinances and your local natural heritage sites and make sure they are protected. Take photographs of these sites, and label their locations. Present your findings to your local government council. Request that they put in place protective laws.

Portal Problems

There is a very interesting grass vortex along the path of a local woodland nature preserve in Illinois—the same preserve mentioned in "Mafia Hit Man" (chapter 1). The path cuts through one side of the vortex, and in the middle of the vortex is a single tree. Unlike the magnolia vortex in the preceding story, here the vortex has pushed aside the energies passing through its area so that the passing energies are stacked around the edge of the vortex. This is similar to the way a pencil poked through the weave of a sweater pushes the weave aside, compressing it around the pencil. The rim energies are so compressed that the plants growing inside that rim are contorted. Tangled vines grow on trees, and some trees are so affected they ended up growing along the ground, unable to rise up.

When I returned from the visit to Swarthmore mentioned in the last story, I was on the lookout for other tree portal sites that had the three components (base location, stabilizing object, and vesica pisces). When I stepped inside this vortex, next to the center tree, and looked about, my attention was drawn to a tall thin Y-tree through which a vesica pisces of branches could be observed. I tracked the energy line down into the circle. However, its trajectory seemed to end in the ground a few feet in front of the tree and not at the tree itself. There was some sort of disturbed feeling near the center tree.

I visited this site repeatedly, puzzling over the situation, which was quite different from that at Swarthmore. Something was amiss here, and no one was talking!

Finally I began to piece the puzzle together: the natural energies of this location had been tampered with unconsciously. Around the central vortex there was a very distinct border of discordant energy—an eight-foot-wide area that was differentiating what was inside the circle from what was outside. A woodland path cut through the vortex which had weakened its energy, precluding it from fully protecting itself. This was an unstable vortex, and any energy going in or out would have to pass through the tangled frequencies of a significant swath of energy around its border; that could very well throw off the intended aim of an incoming or outgoing life form.

It became clear that something had travelled through the vesica pisces, aiming for the tree, but was thrown off course by the magnetic chaos of the border and had ended up instead in the ground a few feet from its goal. The energies were powerful and not totally of the light, and I did not feel capable at that time of handling the situation myself.

Several weeks later I walked here with three colleagues and explained what I had learned about portals. "Do you notice anything strange?" I asked them.

When the group focused, they all agreed that there was something stuck in the earth. Something had come through the portal with such force that it had slung into the earth and was trapped. We discussed what could be done, each of us silently communing with the situation.

Our decision was to move to the edge of the circle, each of us in a different area, looking out rather than in. We would invoke protection for us all and start clearing the energy of the circle, each in her own way so that whatever was trapped could be released. We each invoked our inner team, and I could feel the energies inside the circle fluctuate. Suddenly there was a very loud clap, like a small explosion, and all the tension inside the circle was released. At that point we turned around, went back into the circle, and saw a huge gash in the earth—at the point where the life form had been trapped.

We never knew what had been released, but from the sound of the explosion and the size of the hole, it was good we had not been watching!

Figure 3.3. The Y-tree and the vesica pisces. Note how much less stable this configuration is than the Swarthmore magnolias.

Earth Energies

Figure 3.4. View from the grounding tree to the edge of the vortex. Note the disturbed tree growth of this area, which indicates the stacking of ley lines around the edge. Note the well-worn path to the left, cutting through the vortex.

Figure 3.5. The energy around the perimeter of the vortex is so stacked, and so discordant, that some trees can only grow along the ground instead of growing up.

127

Figure 3.6. Two of my three colleagues identify with the energies involved.

LESSONS

Portals—also known as gateways, passages, wormholes, vortexes, tunnels, and cords, depending on their specific characteristics—exist throughout creation, potentially wherever two lines of light energy cross and their energies intersect. They affect us in our everyday lives, whether we know it

Figure 3.7. The hole left from the release of the life form. The hole was a few feet from the base of the grounding tree.

or not. We can walk through a vortex and suddenly feel very good or very bad. Vortexes can affect our health and that of our family and land. They can help us move from one dimension to another.

As our world increases in frequency, more and more people are going to become aware of the presence of various types of earth energies, including portals.

You need to learn discernment in working with these energetic devices. Some are benign while others, such as the portal in this story, have problems attached. So please don't go experimenting with portals unless you are with experienced friends or have a close working relationship with your inner team who will alert you if an issue arises.

THE BOG ORB

Several energy-worker colleagues went for a walk in an Illinois forest preserve that circled a very large lake. The preserve had a new highway and housing development on one side of the lake and a very large combination of prairie and rolling woodland on the other side.

One of the hills had two vortexes that counter-rotated to each other and we spent some time in the area exploring this energy configuration. The counter-rotating vortex had dark energy, and the clockwise-rotating vortex had light energy; there was a series of tree trunks that had fallen down between the two.

We finished our explorations and started down the path to find something new. But before long we became aware of a large, dark bulbous form clumping along after us. It had a nagging energy that I found annoying, and finally I turned around and told him to go away. It was a life form I had previously photographed when I sensed its presence between two trees that were about five feet apart and within the positive vortex on the hill. Figure 3.8 shows a very large ball of light—an orb—that entirely filled the space. Whatever the life form was, it was big!

The life form refused to move. He just stood there, his head lowered in heart-breaking sadness. He was so forlorn that our little group

Figure 3.8. The bog orb observing me; he is seen here as a white orb of light between the two trees.

took pity on him, shifted focus, and went into conscious energy worker mode.

"What do you want? I asked.

With great sadness, he explained that he was stranded in our world and wanted to go home. "Please help me," he said.

"What happened?" I asked.

He was not very facile with interdimensional communication—he was simply an "ordinary" life form of his world, so it would be like an "ordinary" human being suddenly sent through a portal into another world and not knowing what that world was about or how to speak its language. In a combination of motioning and transmitting images, he let us know that he was aware we had been doing interdimensional work on his hill and he hoped we might help him.

He informed us that life forms from his world were being sucked into ours when there were loud explosions. And he showed us the type of blasting that is done for road construction—which had been done to build the road on the other side of the lake. He conveyed to us that there was a doorway between his world and ours in the lower part of the detonation range. He demonstrated this, following the sound of the detonation down to a specific low frequency and spreading his hand out to show how that was the frequency the sound resonated along. If the detonation hit that frequency, it would sometimes open a portal into his world. The vacuum pressure would suck into our world any unfortunate life forms from his world who were too close to the tear—as he had been. Then the portal would instantly shut and leave the beings stranded here.

The poor fellow was stuck here; he found our world and our life forms no more attractive than he was to us, and he wanted desperately to go home.

We asked him to explain a bit more so we could get a sense of his energetic situation. He told us that the beings in his world like to be around water, especially bogs, and would locate a quiet area near water to live in. He knew his energy scared humans, so he and his kind, when stuck here, would try to send out a ball of light to disguise their whereabouts. This accounted for the light-colored orb I had photographed.

Although this big fellow looked scary, he was actually quite gentle, benign, and lonely for home. The three of us set space, opened a portal to his world, and he was gone.

LESSONS

Construction on a piece of property can affect many, many families and dimensions of life forms. It would be a great benefit to all if people would respect the resident energies and work with them instead of feeling that they can do as they please with "inanimate" land. Many serious situations that require rectifying could be avoided by sending out the message ahead of time that changes are going to occur. There are energetic guards at all portals, and it is their job to hear such announcements and act to protect their world.

Sudden bursts of energy, such as detonations to move earth at a construction site, can cause a rip or tear in the grids that sustain and separate various worlds. Also during construction, existing grid portals are often bulldozed or built over, causing them to close or malfunction.

In the situation with the bog orb, an explosion had resonated at the same frequency as the portal into the orb's world, which had blown it open, sucked in the energies that were there—like a tornado does in our world—and then, when the sound stopped, slammed it shut. It left the orb on this side of the portal, now securely sealed, with no way home.

The orb soon learned he needed to send out a protective ball of light to disguise himself from the denizens of this world. But this was consciously willed, and when his focus dropped, as when he followed us seeking help, his personal energy field came forward. That frequency was sufficiently heavy and different from ours so that it pushed against our personal energetic fields and made us uneasy.

This is an extreme example of a situation that occurs with humans every day. We are all inherently merkabahs, or orbs of energy. When we push an energy away, instead of transforming it, the rejected energy accrues along the outer edge of our merkabah and becomes what outsiders viewing the field see upon approach. Hence a person who internally is working very hard to master compassion and caring can appear to others as cold and uncaring. That is because the individual is proceeding by not looking at, and pushing aside, anything uncaring in his own nature, instead of looking at and transforming that energy.

In the well-known dowsing book on energy fields by Käthe Bachler, *Earth Radiation*, the author describes her frequency studies of European churches. She found that while the energy inside the churches was very high, lower frequencies were pushed back around the perimeter of the churches, creating a series of rings that were negative in nature. Therefore, it became a type of protection; when people approached, they sensed the negative energy grid and moved aside; only those with a reason for being inside the grid would enter for the sustenance of light that was inside.

Likewise people who are frightened will call in light and push back the darkness, which becomes what outsiders see when looking at them. Although they feel light inside, they project the very thing they are rejecting. A spiritually illumined person has transformed all these dark energies, so when they are approached, their inner light permeates and reaches out in all directions; they have an open, accepting field that nourishes all.

Conversely, people who are calling in and focusing on dark forces often are very charismatic and attract ordinary people, who are then surprised by the darkness of the individual that is later revealed. That is because people focusing on darkness are consciously pushing aside the forces of light, which now accrue around the edges of their merkabahs.

Exercise

Time to practice what happens when you approach different vortexes of energy! You want to discern and be aware of what happens as you approach a vortex, move through its edges, and move into its core energy.

One powerful way to do this is to select two houses of worship in your area—one you have an affinity for and one you do not. Practice approaching these buildings and study what occurs at different points. What happens when you are far away? When do you reach a resistance point where, if you didn't care for the energy inside, you would want to leave, and if you do care for it, you have a different reaction? What are these reactions? Even when you like the denomination, do you still feel a certain resistance you push through to continue on? Does it slow you down? What is the energy like when you move through this barrier and go inside it? If you are permitted to enter the building, do so, and identify with the clear energy of its faith once you are in the vortex itself. Eventually reverse the process and see what occurs as you remove yourself.

How does this help you understand any aversions you have to that faith? Can you teach yourself to be detached as you move through all these separate, differing fields so that you can see into the core essence of the energy itself? It is here, inside the core of the energy, that you can get the true sense of that faith and can test its core values and essence which have been affected by many other energies that are absorbed into its outer layers.

You can test this with other types of buildings that house other powerful energies, such as a courthouse, a school, or a disreputable bar. Testing this on disreputable sites can teach you why disreputable organizations attract the young, naïve, and energetically untrained individuals! As naïve people wander near that organization, which has moved that which is beautiful and elevating to the outside rim of its dark vortex, that beauty attracts the untrained like a magnet! They are sucked in by the beauty, which can serve to disguise that which it is not. This is another reason why energetic training is so important to successful survival in our world!

A FAERY'S WORST OFFENSE

It was a warm, lazy summer day, and I was walking along a woodland path in a local Illinois forest preserve. It was near the start of my interdimensional work. I was crossing a small bridge above a gently flowing stream, the kind of stream that expands to turbulence in early spring, then slows down to a crawl by midsummer. A thin, small voice called out: "Help!" I stopped, looked around, but saw nothing.

"Help me!" I heard again.

I looked about for the source of the sound. To my left, downstream, was the skeleton of a tree that had toppled some years before in a spring flood. The roots were facing me and when I looked carefully, I saw tangled in amongst them a fairy. He looked like the classic image of a prisoner of the old days: wild disheveled hair streaming out all around, sunken features, and a skeletal body.

I was quite taken aback and didn't know what to make of it all. The fairy wanted me to come free him, but something was wrong with the situation. I decided the best course of action was to walk on, ask my team what was occurring, and wait for their response. I've learned caution is the best course of action in a situation such as this!

I completed one circuit of the two-mile preserve path and began another round. As I approached the stream and was wondering what to do, a powerful devic voice spoke to me.

"Don't help him," it said.

"Why?" I asked, stopping abruptly.

The deva explained that the fairy had been in charge of the tree in which he was now trapped. The tree had been tall, magnificent, and occupied a key vortex point for clearing and stabilizing that area's energy grid. But the tree fairy had been negligent and irresponsible in the fulfillment of his duties. Because of this, during a storm, his tree had fallen over far before its time. This had left the area weak and unprotected, causing many problems as the mature devas worked hard to build up another vortex holding point. For this serious dereliction of duty, the fairy was being punished by being imprisoned in the tree. It was a lesson for him and for the other tree spirits as well.

"Is he there for eternity?" I asked.

"No," the deva explained. "He has a specific time frame for his sentence."

I thanked the deva for the information and walked on.

That weekend I was visiting with my brother Chet, who had walked in this preserve for years. When I described the incident, he replied, "I always wondered about that! That was the most glorious tree, and I always paused to admire it. Then one spring it went down in the storms, and I could never figure out why. It had been so strong and healthy!"

When I walked the path over the next two years, the fairy was always there. Then I moved and when I returned for a visit, some three years later, the fairy was gone. His sentence had ended.

LESSONS

The worst offense of nature fairies is dereliction of duty. If, because of their lack of diligence, their plant or tree dies, they are punished. In this situation, the tree was a nodal point for that area, a linchpin in the energy grid. So the resident fairy's irresponsibility had even broader implications than usual for the entire energy of the land. That is why his punishment was so severe.

As you learn to be aware of energy, you have to learn the wisdom of pausing and considering before acting. There are always at least two sides to every story and the work of an earth steward necessitates uncovering the full story rather than a one-sided opinion.

Portals to Other Worlds

During a pleasant meander along the paths of a local Fox River valley park, lined with mature old trees, the resident deva directed me to a small hillock and a group of three cottonwood trees. "These are the alpha trees of the area," she informed me, "the ones in charge of the others."

Cottonwood trees are considered one of the most significant trees by the Native Americans of the plains states. They are soft, gentle community trees. They have heart-shaped leaves that move even when there appears to be no breeze, thus serving as a wind path to the gods. Cottonwood tree spirits have the ability to answer questions and solve problems and help one transition into other worlds. They have many images in their roots and trunks that can serve as message conveyers for the energy they are holding inside their space.

Around the base of this trio of cottonwood trees there were three exposed roots that had formed into round holes, or portals, as the devas explained it. The portals were gentle spirit gateways into other worlds. They covered three frequencies: the mind (there was a set shaped like eyes), the heart (there was a heart-shaped root), and the body (there was a large round hole, like a base chakra at the base of a human body, and this portal combined or harmonized both male and female sexual organs).

The heart portal was large enough for a person to sit in. It had a round "flower" that could meet the base of the backbone, a key kundalini area for absorbing energy into the body. The deva suggested I first look into the portal to assure myself it was safe to use. When I did this, I was shown a route deep into the heart of the earth; it was soothing, refreshing, and illuminating. So I sat on the portal and relaxed into a wonderful experience of being enveloped by earth energy.

I enjoyed the experience so much that I requested permission of the deva to bring a group of workshop attendees to experience the portal. She consented. The workshop attendees all had wonderful experiences as well. Interestingly, a long-time practicing yogi was in the class. He looked into the portal, traveling deep inside the earth and then out into the cosmos where he experienced great peace and openness.

I have shown a photo of this portal at various workshops and asked participants to identify with its energy. This is as effective as an in-person experience, and the range of responses replicates those of people visiting the site.

Figure 3.9. The heart portal—part of a root of the alpha cottonwood tree.

Figure 3.10. The alpha trees, with the heart portal root at their base (circled). Note the graffiti on the tree. I learned from this desecration not to identify locations on my photographs. Doing so leaves the sites open to abuse, perhaps not by the people visiting the site for inspiration, but by the people walking by observing those working at the area. Some humans perversely destroy what they do not understand. Fortunately, these markings eventually wore off.

Figure 3.11. To comprehend these energies more clearly, I created a collage of the portals, lining them up in human body order, overlapping the tree itself.

LESSONS

The devas throughout this park are actively working to develop peaceful cooperation among naturally competing energies. What is the history and energy in your local parks? How can you work with this to assist yourself and your community?

The history of this park shows why it is interested in cooperation. At one time, it was inhabited by the local Potawatomi peoples. As European settlers moved in, the Potawatomi chose to live in cooperation with the settlers, protected them from the antagonistic Fox tribes of the area, and finally left the area with a blessing that the whites would enjoy the land as much as they had. This is a true testament to the peaceful spirit of that nation!

Next, this park area was open-pit mined by early settlers for stone for buildings. When the pits got too deep and mining stopped, the land lay like an open eyesore. Then the community got together and filled in the pit and built a park on the land for the enjoyment of all.

So the current park's nature spirits have experienced harmony, abuse, and restoration. They are knowledgeable and have the ability to talk about forgiveness and harmony among opposing forces. Their trees often contain images of those who are natural competitors, such as male/female and animals who are often the predator and the hunted. Their trees are part of the healing that the spirits profoundly offer the local community.

There are many active root portals in a variety of trees, each with its own energy and entry point to a variety of other worlds. Identifying with these trees can help humans move into a state of cooperation with their own internally competing energies!

SINKHOLES AND TREE MERIDIANS

Sometimes, when I'm stressed from work, I will place my hands on a pine tree trunk and request the tree spirit to run its soothing sap-like energy through mine, to clear and ground my energy field. Pine trees are very good aligners of electromagnetic energy and are an excellent buffer in EMF-polluted areas.

However, on one occasion, when I walked through a small, local pine forest, I had a different experience. When I approached a pine tree, placed my hands on it, and made my respectful request, nothing happened. No energy flowed through me.

From behind my back, a nature spirit gently spoke. "You're too stressed and too clogged up; the pine tree can't move any energy through you," the spirit said. My heart sank; this was a new one! What was I to do now?

"Turn around. There's another solution," the spirit responded to my thoughts.

I did as requested but saw nothing.

"Now look down," the spirit said.

When I did, I saw a small sinkhole about two feet from the tree. It was three feet across, twelve inches deep in its center area, and partially filled with leaves from nearby trees. It had a dark, astringent energy.

We don't have a lot of sinkholes in the northeast area of the USA where I was raised, so I was unfamiliar with their features. They are common in the Midwest Great Lakes region where there is a lot of soft limestone that erodes easily and the water table is close to the surface. That can be a difficult situation in your yard, so a lot of people keep filling sinkholes in. But here they were located in the middle of a forest preserve, hence untouched.

The nature spirit explained that this sinkhole also functioned as a negative vortex. I identified this concept with the "black water" that dowsers talk about that can affect land energy. I looked at the sinkhole with curiousity and noticed it had a strong counterclockwise spin and a minor clockwise spin within it.

"This vortex lives on negative energy," said the spirit, "and this makes it very useful for clearing any piece of property, and humans as well. Go stand in the vortex," the nature spirit instructed me. "Take all your negative energy and stress and consciously send it down into the vortex. Everyone will benefit from this! The vortex will be fed the type of energy it needs, and you will be cleared. Then you can go to the pine tree, and it can assist you."

I scanned for any possible disguised motives on any life form's part, found none, asked my team for protection, and decided to give it a try.

I stepped into the depression and stood still. Gradually I felt all the stress of the past few weeks drain through my feet, down through the sinkhole and deep into the earth herself. I could sense it going into the deep pool of energy at the core center of the earth consciousness—that amalgam where all energies bubble and boil together, available for our use as needed. I didn't need these negative energies anymore, and the earth was taking them back.

It became very silent inside my energy field as all the noise of the disappearing discordant energy drained out. I was cleared, but not yet energized.

"Now go to the pine tree," the nature spirit said.

I did as requested and placed both hands on the pine tree trunk. I felt the pine tree welcome me, then pour that wonderfully soft, gentle, rejuvenating energy through my nervous system. It felt like the tree's sap, flowing through its energy meridians, was merging with and flowing through mine! All was now right again in my world! I thanked the spirits profusely and continued on my walk.

On future trips to this preserve, the nature spirits taught me more about these phenomena. There were three sinkholes in that immediate area, lined up in a row in front of three pine trees. These three trees were very straight and strong while many others in the area were curved or leaning. Each of these energy pairs (tree and sinkhole) was working at a different frequency—low, medium, or high. They were like energetic sand paper. One cleared the big stuff, the next refined the clearing, and the third did the final polishing. The combination kept the ley line the trees were on very clear and straight, and I could track its effect for hundreds of yards on either side.

Figure 3.12. Three sinkholes and the pine trees they work with.

Lessons

The round sinkholes present on many properties in the Great Lakes prairie region unfortunately are not widely appreciated. In this area, the water table is very close to the surface, and the pull from earth shifts and underground streams often cause depressions in the surface land.

Many people have sinkhole areas on their property and most keep filling them in with new soil each spring, to achieve a smooth lawn. It is beneficial to work with the energy that causes the sinkhole. A sinkhole is a negative vortex area. When surrounded by thorny plants or a rose bush, or next to a pine tree, it becomes doubly effective as a natural negative energy drain for that property.

Pine trees are an excellent addition for any work with electromagnetic fields and are associated with the energy of long life, creative flow, and immortality. Their long needles are representative of the type of energy that they "run" through themselves: a straight, astringent flow. They work well when planted around a home to clear its energetic perimeter. They work well with humans, running cleansing energy through your field like an electromagnetic-releasing brush and hose.

Connecting to tree energy is an excellent remedy to know about if you travel a lot overseas. However, you also have to be consciously aware of the willingness of the natural site to work with you.

During the part of my life when I traveled a great deal, I sometimes would eat something that did not agree with me. My inner team taught me a remedy: locate a strong local tree, place my hands on it, and request it to run its clearing local earth energy through mine. This clears you out, adapts you to local microbes, and energizes you.

The local trees were almost always very accommodating. However, once I encountered the only condescending trees I have ever met. It was when I was in Tokyo, had eaten something wrong, and was walking through the Imperial Palace gardens. There was a grove of beautiful pine trees, and I decided to ask their help. But as soon as I entered the grove, its presiding nature spirit spoke to me very condescendingly: "WHO are you, and WHAT do you want!" It quite unnerved me to be spoken to that way by trees, but I was quite ill and needed help so I braved on, described my plight, and requested their help. There was a long silence. Then, finally, a condescending but accepting response: "Well, all right, just this once. But DON'T COME BACK!" I thanked them, placed my hands on the trunk of a pine, and felt its clearing life-force energy flow through me. I left, fully recovered.

But two days later my conscience was hurting me. My guides had taught me to always offer thanks when I have been helped, so I decided I had better go back and do so. I returned to the royal gardens and entered the pine grove. The reaction was immediate: the nature spirit announced loudly and condescendingly: "We TOLD YOU not to come back!" With that I apologized profusely, said I was just returning to thank them, did so, backed out of the grove, and did not ever return!

EXERCISE

Take a walk in nature or in your own yard. Locate a tree that especially appeals to you. Go up to it and request that it connect to your energy field and feed its soothing life force sap through yours, to clear and reenergize you. Then, as the situation and your instincts allow, either place both hands on the tree, lean your back against the tree, or sit at the base of the tree and allow the tree energy to flow through you.

Second exercise: take a walk, locate an area with a sinkhole or a place in your yard that you are continually filling in. Ask permission to step inside this vortex to release your own tensions. If you feel an accepting response, step inside. Stand straight, and feel energy flowing down through the top of your head and out through your feet, down through the sinkhole and into the center of the earth. You may feel a counterclockwise flow or a simple downward pull. Take all of your anxieties, worries, and tension, and send them down into the hole. Then stand still and enjoy the peace. Thank the spirit of the vortex and step out. You have done a service to the world, for you have activated a natural energy-releasing site and fed it the energy it needs to continue to serve!

Negative and Positive Vortexes

David and Pam had built a ceremonial fire pit at the back of their property, locating it according to the instructions of a local shaman. Next to it was a large patch of wild raspberry bushes whose energy was bothering the couple. "We had a fire ceremony two days ago, and in spite of our best efforts, we can feel everyone's released debris floating above these bushes! There's such negative energy in this briar area," Pam said, "we're considering ripping out the bushes!"

The minute I turned my attention to the briar bushes, the raspberry sprites began complaining to me about the humans! "We're trying to do our job," they insisted, "and the land owners are sending out thought forms that block us!"

If they were not so distressed by this situation, I would have laughed, for there were innumerable raspberry sprites whirring about in a dither of distress, crowding about me to be heard as soon as they discovered I was aware of them.

"Tell these humans to stop interfering with our work," they pleaded.

I explained the situation to the owners. "This area is actually a strong asset for your spiritual purpose, and it would be even more valuable if you consciously directed to the bushes the negative energy being drained off of people during fire ceremony or even during contemplative sessions at the site."

Once the couple understood the situation, they were more than willing to adjust their perceptions and to value this area. The three of us then worked cooperatively with the bushes to create an energy funnel that would direct the negative energy released during ceremony or meditative contemplation into the bushes.

In this situation, the fire ceremony was working as a positive vortex, spinning out clearing energy in a clockwise manner. The briar bushes were working as a negative vortex, drawing in negative energy in a counterclockwise manner. Such a pairing of energies frequently occurs, especially in spiritually active areas.

With both vortexes now working, the area itself thrived, and the air again became sparkling clear, just as the owners wished.

Lessons

Briar bushes and other such thorny plants gravitate to and do well in areas of negative energy. They can be extremely useful devices for keeping the energy of a property clear and balanced.

A negative vortex is one in which energy spins out, counterrotating to the dominant life force of that field.

The precise definition of "negative" takes its form from its relationship to the full field. Negative vortexes are very useful devices for balancing and clearing area energy. Don't automatically assume such a site should be destroyed.

Very often, negative vortexes are paired with positive ones to balance the energies in a location. The problem comes when either vortex is clogged or imbalanced. The appropriate procedure is to clear and balance both, so that they can function appropriately in relation to each other.

In our Western society, one land-balancing issue comes from the insistence that everything on the property has to be "good" and anything negative must be "destroyed." A property owner's pursuit of this—for example, leveling sinkholes or fertilizing areas where grass won't grow—is actually causing imbalance. They have pitted themselves in an unconscious battle with the nature forces of that property. These forces are struggling to retain the health of the area in spite of human interference.

Once the landowners learn how they are misperceiving the situation and how to connect with the energies of their property, they are usually very willing and ready to work in harmony with the nature spirits. When this is done, the owners—and sometimes the spirits as well—report the energetic situation at that site has greatly improved.

The nature spirits were very active on the site, working with the owners to enhance and augment the energies. But even so, if the concept is one that humans do not know about, it is often difficult for the nature spirits to effect the proper change. If humans do not believe the situation is a possibility, it means they have not opened themselves to the frequency on which the situation is communicating. The humans either cannot "hear" the solution at all, or they block it as false information. This, by the way, is one of the reasons why some energy workers exchange sessions with each other: to learn other ways of seeing into the vast universe of possibilities in which we live and to locate the "blind spots" that are causing them personal problems.

PHOTOGRAPHS

You can understand more about the energy of your own property or area by studying the condition of your plants. Walk around your yard. Where are there bare patches in the grass that just won't grow no matter how many times you reseed? Where are dead spots in bushes? What is the shape of the trees around your house? Do they lean at an angle? Is that angle explained by growth around them, or can you sight along the trees and see a whole line of trees in either direction that are at an angle, indicating some energy the trees are growing around.

There are vortexes and ley lines throughout earth. Learn what is happening on your property so that you can make adjustments or adapt around the energies and thus ensure the health of all in your home.

If there are negative spots, should these be removed or utilized?

Photograph those spots demonstrating extreme energy of a positive or negative order. When you download these photographs onto your computer, use the exposure/curves/level tools to clarify the energies that are subtly present.

Archive these photos, and reshoot at different times of the day and night, in different seasons and times of the month, to understand if the energies are seasonal, cyclical, or continual. Study the energy shifts over time as you work to adjust them. This documentation becomes a visual proof of your ability to work cooperatively with nature.

Chapter 3

GIVE US BACK GANESH!

Some years ago, I bought an older ranch house in St. Charles, Illinois, and happily moved in. The former owners were very jovial, very nice sports trainers. I set up a home office in the master bedroom and turned the small second bedroom next to it into my bedroom. My desk and my bed had only one logical location—on the same north/south line and parallel to each other in an east/west direction. But I did not feel comfortable in either room. There was a definite line of energy cutting right through these two significant locations, north to south. I called upon all my tools with no success and then tried connecting to the energy, but I could not locate its frequency. It was a powerful, established line of energy that I could not comprehend but that made me so uncomfortable that it was affecting my health.

Finally, I took the matter to my team, and, in a most insistent manner, requested help. It actually took me several years to fully understand what was going on because of my entrenched opinions; I was not totally detached from the solution to the problem, so could not clearly see the solution. It is sometimes difficult for your inner team to assist you in a situation such as this—they can offer solutions that you can follow without understanding why, and when they try to explain, they come up against your blind spots which prevent you from seeing and hearing.

I finally came to understand that a teaching ley line was passing through my desk and my bed. I am also a teacher, of esoteric topics, and at the time I was still seeking to balance the rules of many dimensions, in order to see accurately. I had learned that the rules for one dimension or group within a society are not necessarily the rules for another dimension or group. To successfully travel through worlds, one must be willing to adjust to the different parameters developed by each group to meet its differently evolving needs. However, along this ley line there were a number of points of very set and unwavering frequency that came from teaching establishments that believed theirs was the way, and the only way, to solve issues. This point of view results in unending battles for supremacy of viewpoint.

There were too many of these frequencies vying for control for me to process, so my body would shut down.

I finally drove out in my car and tracked the line. The north/south line of energy began two miles to the north—at the altar of a very conservative church, then out the front door, through a secondhand "antique store," through a series of physical fences separating yards, through an abandoned middle school, through more physical fences, through a very large ground generator about one-quarter mile from my house, through a series of backyard fences, through my house which had been owned by muscle-sculpting teachers, through more yards, and ending a mile away at a high school. So the line looked like a bunch of crosshatches, all crossing the ley line at physical levels.

My team asked me what a positive solution would be. When I could not think of any, they inwardly showed me an image of the very large bronze Indian statue of Ganesh that I owned. Ganesh is a Hindu god—a cosmic energy—who embodies good luck, prosperity, and who is also a patron to writers and speakers; he is one of my favorite energies, because I am a writer and a small business owner. Ganesh's energy of creativity, his wide acceptance of all points of view, and his embodiment of happy cosmic energies would strengthen and stabilize these frequencies along that line.

The team asked me to put Ganesh on a south-side shelf in my office, right on the ley line, and to place simple offerings at the shrine to strengthen Ganesh's energy. I did so, and the energy along the line as it passed through my property instantly changed. I had no more problems. With the help of my inner team, I had found a way to insert an energy node with a frequency that was more compatible to mine into the prevailing ley line.

Well, I thought that was that, and the energy had been permanently corrected. However, several years later, I opened a new store and "borrowed" the large Ganesh statue from my house to bless the store. All was well for a time, but then the energy in my house started changing. I tried various remedies and finally sat down and conversed with it at a serious level. The house energy informed me it was very, very angry with me, and I definitely felt its anger! It said I was ignoring it, not giving it enough importance now that I had merged the home business into the new store. But, most importantly, it said it wanted Ganesh to come back home and be put back in its place. It could not hold the energies Ganesh had been holding for the house.

I agreed, brought Ganesh back, put him in his place, and all the house energies rushed in to greet him. It was a very happy reunion, and I could feel the joy of all levels of the nature spirits on my property. Over the next few days, the energies of the property moved back into a much more positive range. Early one morning, a whole flutter of tiny faeries woke me up to thank me for bringing Ganesh back to them.

LESSONS

This experience made me very aware of the interconnectedness of all the energies working at different frequencies on a piece of land. It also made me aware of how statues, drawings, and photographs can embody the energy of the object they portray and how they can come awake and affect the energy of the space in which they rest.

If a corrective tool is put along a line to change it on a local level, then it needs to be checked occasionally to make certain it is still functioning. Sometimes the corrective tool adapts to the prevailing energy and is no longer effective. In the case of the statue, it ties into a morphogenetic field of the Ganesh energy around the world. When such energy is locally awakened, it will be continuously active. If the tool is removed, as when I removed the Ganesh statue from my home, the other active frequencies will naturally start filling in the void. This is something Dr. Masaru Emoto discovered in his experiments with clearing water, such as in the Great Lakes. While he was able to clear the water with prayer, when he returned a year later, he discovered the lake was once again polluted. This was because polluted water kept pouring into the lake from other sources, and no one was saying prayers to keep the collective area clear.

How Trees Hold Space

There is an alpha tree (like an alpha dog) for each nature area, and he/she connects to other trees in that area and to other trees in other sectors. These trees, even in death, will stay in place and be populated by the local devas, who continue to hold space until they can develop another linchpin.

When humans wantonly invade a piece of property and cut down everything in a wide swath to put up housing or shopping developments, they do devastating harm to the natural order of the area that has been so carefully developed by nature spirits over the course of millennia.

Trees and rocks don't usually move, so they develop faces, which embody the various energies they are holding for that area. Trees and rocks are much more advanced than we humans in their ability to connect to different frequencies. They are sometimes node points on grids spanning the earth and may have images of animals or cultures half a world away. They also connect to multiple dimensions and may have images of nature spirits or life forms of parallel earths in their faces.

Sometimes the only way to illustrate the complex energy of such trees is through photographic collages. Following are two collages that show the very rich and aware nature life that is going on around us every day.

The collage in Figure 3.13 shows three versions of the same tree over five years. This is a "collage of time." The left image shows the tree five years ago when it was a lively "flirt," the right image shows the tree now, looking like an old crone, and in the middle image I photographically merged the two to indicate a transition phase. In the right image, the tree has physically died, but it still houses nature spirits because it serves as the alpha tree for its area. It will continue to house the spirits until they fashion a new tree in that area to serve as a linchpin in the overall land grid.

Examining these images more closely, we see that the tree on the left was photographed in the spring, at a stage five years before the photo on the right. At the upper left you can see a close-up of the tree's face. It is that of a flirt—long eyelashes, pursed mouth, come-hither arms. She wants to draw energies to the rich swampy lowland over which she presides, and

Figure 3.13. Time collage of tree.

the area and stream she is next to are well populated with birds and small animals.

To the right is the tree in the late fall, five years later, now physically dead but energetically still alive. You can see a close-up of her face at the bottom right—it is that of a wrinkled old crone. The flirt has grown old, as all flirts do, and the weathering of the seasons has reduced the tree in size—"stunted" her—from the top down. The image now is of an old hag who wants to be left alone!

Under the right arm of the old crone tree is the Green Faery orb who frequently appears when I get my best interdimensional nature photographs. I placed that arm and orb over the center image, where I combined the two photographs to show the tree in transition between the two stages. The Green Faery is an essential part of my ability to move into the right space to get good nature photographs; she permeates nature as Archangel Michael does in the angelic realms!

Because this so-called dead old crone tree is a key linchpin in the area's grid, nature spirits are still occupying her, to sustain the grid itself. To understand how linchpin trees connect to one another over different nature sectors, look at the collage below, which is a "collage of space."

This collage below shows two nodes on the earth grid connecting to each other. In the distant middle is the tree shown above, as it looks today. In the front is a burr oak, located on a cliff at the other side of the swampy valley. The burr oak serves as the node point for its part of that area's nature grid. The burr oak has a bear image burr, and I show a close-up of that bear burr at the far left.

Linchpins on their swamp grid, these two trees have been facing each other for a hundred years or more, helping to hold the energy for the area. They are not mates but colleagues; the bear tree's mate—his female aspect—is a large burr oak just out of sight behind him. Looking at this collage, you can see why the nature spirits are still occupying the physically dead old crone tree; she is essential to the healthy maintenance of that area.

(There is a winter close-up of the bear burr [Figure 0.8.] in the introduction to this book.)

Figure 3.14. Space collage of trees.

LESSONS

As nature becomes used to you and you prove yourself to be trustworthy and useful to the local deva's agenda, more and more is revealed to you. Until you progress to the next step in your learning, you are very happy where you are. But once you cross each line of understanding and your consciousness opens up another notch, you again marvel at the infinite profundity of this amazing universe. To think that humans are the only ones who have been evolving in this universe is wrong. All the different worlds are evolving, each in its own way according to its own rules. The intricate way in which nature has evolved solutions to its issues of surviving, thriving, success, propagation, and service is a wonder.

EXERCISE

Practice sitting and observing the natural world around you, wherever you may be. As you learn to see the trees, plants, rocks, and animals with clear eyes, reach out to them silently, peacefully, and with the intent of non-harm. Envision yourself as simply one part of the broad community of life forms who inhabit this earth. Do the other life forms want to share their life knowledge with you? Are they offering you help in some way? Do they require your assistance in some way? Find some action in which you and the life forms of that area can cooperate. Do your part to fulfill that action. Observe how your understanding of our common existence improves through such service.

PHOTOGRAPHS

My advice to aspiring nature spirit photographers: be persistent. Keep going back to a favorite area, and keep requesting assistance from the local nature spirits to help you record their presence. I happen to love the energy of the burr oak shown in this chapter and have gone back to sit with it over and over. Gradually, as the nature locale comes to know and trust you, the spirits will be more inclined to reveal themselves in their grand complexity.

The two collages in this section show the value of photographing and archiving your photographs so that you have documentation of the changes nature creates over time.

· 4 ·

Rock, Tree, and Faery Spirits

GRANDFATHER ROCK

One October, about the time I had just begun studying earth energies, I was vending my energy products and gemstone prayer beads at a yoga conference high in the Rocky Mountains, at Estes Park, Colorado. It was a beautiful setting—a peaceful volcanic valley ringed by snow-covered mountains. I was contemplating some radical lifestyle changes, and the accompanying inner turmoil was such that during a break in the conference, while attendees were focused on hatha yoga, I escaped for a walk in the forest.

My feet took me to a hillside strewn with boulders large and small, and the prevailing stone energy was so soothing that I sought an appropriate place to sit and center. Guided to a large, peaceful boulder, I sat in yogic cross-legged style in a cubbyhole at its base and entered into meditation. Very soon my turmoil abated as a firm, gentle stone energy drew me deep down into the middle of the earth where I felt comforted and safe, surrounded by many of the stone spirits of that location. When I came back up, all my energies were at peace, and I was filled with renewed strength to go forward.

Figure 4.1. Grandfather rock, Estes Park, Colorado. The cubby area is in the shadow space beneath his eye.

I had been led to sit at the base of Grandfather—the head of the extended family of rocks that spread out over an acre of land. Grandfather made me an honorary member of his family, and over the rest of that visit and for many years after, I would return, first during the yoga conferences and then just to say hello. A huge photograph of Grandfather now rests over the door to my rock shop.

When a site has at least one strong image in a tree or rock—such as Grandfather—I will usually find many other images, or energies, also present. The site serves as a portal between the two worlds of nature and humanity. The variety of forms in that area depends on the energy it is holding; it could be connected to sites in other parts of the globe, or to a particular aspect of human energy that resides there now or did so in the past. If the spirits find you worthy and in resonance with them, such a place is a good one in which to interact in a communal fashion.

The rock spirits of that area adopted me into their family, and over time I got to know many of them. They include a protective grandmother and

Figure 4.2. Grandma rock (right) and baby (middle). Grandma faces Grandfather, across a sunny open area.

Figure 4.3. The bird family: a chauvinistic old grouch (facing left) and behind him, to the right, his abused wife with wing raised to protect herself.

Figure 4.4. The elephant rock

Figure 4.5. The bird warrior, in armor.

her mischievous grandchild, a cranky old chauvinistic bird rock and his abused wife, a handsome hero, and elephants, birds, animals, and fish.

There is also an abandoned Native American altar in the area and another one at the base of the hill. The altar at the base of the hill borders a rushing stream and has a snake-energy head, as do many of the old Native American altars. The nature spirits of that area asked me to help them by cleaning natural debris that had settled there. On my subsequent visits, I always made certain to do a bit of altar cleansing, as an offering to spirit.

For many years, I wondered why these altars would show a snake with only one eye. Finally a Native American explained to me that one eye indicates the snake has one part of its consciousness on earth and the other in spirit; it therefore serves to transport someone or something from earth to the realm of spirit.

Figure 4.6. The abandoned altar, near a rushing stream.

Figure 4.7. The snake head of the altar. Photo is shot looking from the stream back. Note one eye open, to left; vertical nose bridge and horizontal mouth, to right.

Figure 4.8. At the end of my last photographic outing at Estes Park, I said good-bye to my stone friends because I might not get back out there again. I looked down and saw their response back: this heart, formed from lichen that had grown over a small rock.

LESSONS

Rocks can manifest images of the energy that they want to embody and hold for an area. Rocks are the original life forms on earth, and their function is to hold energy stable for other life forms to utilize and grow upon. Like trees, some will manifest many faces within the same rock while others will have one predominant image.

Some areas are more intensely populated with these interactive energies than others, and the area around Estes Park and the Rocky Mountain National Park are rich with images. Other rock-energy–rich areas I have personally explored are Sedona, Arizona; southern Illinois; and the White Mountains of New Hampshire. There is a reason why these scenic areas are known for their restorative energies, and that comes from the very active nature world in which rocks play a prominent role.

Not only can you see forms in these rocks, you can communicate with their very different energies. In the rock family described above, the personalities are well developed and differentiated.

As we move into the Age of Spirituality, we will be discovering that it is beneficial for humans to dialogue and cooperate with the stones, trees, and plants of their area before beginning to build. In this way we can maximize the benefits of worlds that have evolved over millions of years, to support and augment our contributions to our common earth. These natural life forms are also of tremendous benefit on a personal level, as each of us works to stabilize positive natural energies in ourselves.

EXERCISE

Native Americans and other Native cultures around the world will often return to nature when they seek an answer they cannot fathom. Here's an exercise for you to try.

Go to a local nature preserve—or your own property, if it is a large one—and sit quietly, centering yourself. Formulate the precise question you need a response to from the universe. This is important: the universe is very pragmatic and literal, and it will respond to the question it perceives you are actually posing even if it is not what you intended—as illustrated by an old dowsing story:

The dowser was demonstrating to an audience how to use dowsing rods to find directions. He asked the rods to show him north. But the rods kept pointing to the left when the dowser knew the direction north was straight ahead. He apologized to the audience—he didn't know what was going on. Then a man in the audience, sitting to the left, spoke up. "Actually," he said, "the dowsing rods are accurate. My name is Bill North!"

So . . . carefully formulate your question. Then request Mother Nature to show you the answer via a stone. Start walking in whatever direction you feel called to. When you feel a stone "pop" out calling to you, pick it up. Sit down if possible or stand quietly and relax into the energy of the stone. Turn it over and about. When an image emerges—some way in which the lines or bumps on the stone stand out—look at that scene and hear/see/feel/perceive (however your energy works) what the message is. When you are finished, you can either return the stone to the earth or take it with you as a physical reminder of the solution.

PHOTOGRAPHS

In areas with strong rock energy, the rocks have developed many different faces as they've physically evolved different energies that they seek to embody. Sometimes these faces will not be recognizable to humans; other times they are very clear. When you are in the mood to see these faces, they will appear many places; when you are not in the mood, or have not sought to identify with the stone energies, they are not observable at all.

The camera, not having a strong emotional body as humans do, primarily records what it sees within its frequency range. As mentioned earlier, the camera is strongly influenced by its user. When photographers are focused on recording the life force energy of the stone or rock, and have an affinity for this form of energy, the camera will often record it even if the photographers cannot see it with their physical eyes. That this is a personal interaction has been demonstrated in several of the nature spirit photography workshops I have hosted. In these workshops, we will have a number of photographers focus in the same direction and take photographs of the same scene. We are working digitally so can see the results immediately on the screen on the back of the camera. We will immediately see that different photographers, with their different orientations, will call forth different energies. Within the same group, we will see the cameras of some people photograph orbs while the cameras of others photograph plasma, auras, and/or physical manifestations.

The only way you can learn what you can do is to start practicing! Take your camera out on a nature shoot. Early morning or late afternoon are very good times for this, as the light is softer, permitting the subtle life forms to be seen more easily. As you enter the area you wish to photograph, pause and address the nature spirit energy of that area. Speak respectfully and ask for its assistance as you work to locate and photograph nature spirit. The energies are alive and can assist you or hinder you! You must hold in your consciousness the awareness that all nature is alive, can communicate, and is meant to work with humans for the benefit of all on earth. Communicate your wish to be able to clearly document this reality for all humans to see.

Now walk about until you find a rock whose energy you are fond of. Stand there for a time; identify with its energy. Then request that it permit you to photograph this energy to share with humans. Addressing your camera, request that it take the appropriate image. Then start photographing. Try different shutter speeds and different apertures if you are shooting on manual. Try shooting up close and far away. Use a steady hand or a tripod. Move about the rock, looking carefully up and down to locate any hidden angles or images.

When you return home and download your images, ask your own inner team as well as the spirit of the rocks and the spirit of the camera to show you where the best images exist. You can zoom in as needed. Be sure you store your images in a safe place. At the start of my own photography, there was many a time I came back later to a collection and found images I hadn't been able to see before. Also, as both my own skills and camera technology developed, I found I had the skills to sharpen a photo or lighten only certain parts of an image taken in deep shadows, and this made the image more clearly visible to others.

Finally, thank all the energies involved, identify with the results so that you can more easily do such photography in the future, and print or upload to share your images with others. Please send your photos to our blog—crystal-life.com/blog—where we share nature images taken by our friends.

Moss Faeries—Maine

The Maine conference campground was rich with the scent of pine woods and fields of tall golden grass. The nature spirits were at their full summer strength, abundantly present and calling to each other as the full moon approached in two nights.

I was at a healing arts conference to present a workshop on interdimensional consciousness. This was near the start of my professional practice, when I was focused primarily on ley lines and land energy.

But here the nature spirits were dominant and they wanted to play! I rose early and went for a walk in the pine forest.

Along the woodland path there was an especially pretty area where rich green moss covered a medley of tree roots, with many small "houses" tucked among them. These houses belonged to the moss faeries of this area. I especially love moss faeries and sent them greetings and appreciation as I passed by.

Next on the walk was a glade of fern fairies. This sunlit area was situated to the right of the path and was ringed by trees. It was impeccably maintained and vibrant with energy! Fern fairies have a delicate energy and tinkling communal sunlit laughter that can send joy clear through a human's energy field!

To the left was a softly rising hill and a second moss faery domain. As it had rather messy energy, I ignored it and focused on the fern glen. The fairies and I had a delicate, tinkling talk about how they live and practice their craft in their particular glen. They showed me how nature spirits work in a circle, which has a "sweet spot" somewhere in the middle that energizes that domain. They helped me sense how a significant change in vibration occurs as the end of each domain is reached. They explained how each area in the forest has its own special energy, which comes in part from the collective focus of the nature spirits living there. Here, the fern spirits were especially artistic so they emphasized that aspect of their world.

As I said good-bye and started to walk on, my attention was caught by a small male moss faery sitting cross-legged, dejectedly pouting. His arms were crossed, and his chin rested in his left hand. He was partway up the mossy hill, sitting on what looked like, from my angle, a tangle of woodland debris. He was clearly very frustrated.

"What's the matter?" I asked, feeling like I was talking to one of my sons when they were children.

"I need help, and no one will listen to me!" he responded.

"Well, I'm listening," I said, "so tell me."

"This place is SO messy!"

I laughed. Now it felt like I had entered never-never land and was talking to a mischievous Peter Pan! "Well, you could try picking it up, like the fairies in the fern glen."

"No," he responded. "You don't understand. I can't do it myself, and I need it fixed!" He pouted and nodded with his head to the debris on which he was sitting.

"Well," I responded, "what do you want me to do?"

"Just come here and see," he said.

Something about the request bothered me; something was being hidden. Having recently encountered problems from entering a nature circle I had not studied first, I knew there can be energies trapped in a circle who one would not want to connect to. I responded that I would think about it and continued on my walk, communicating along the way with a number of other types of woodland spirits, including some mature pines nearby. Tree spirits have the ability to move out of their trees and take a separate form, should they so wish. Here, the spirits presented themselves as a council of tall grey-bearded wise men. They conveyed to me the energy of being solemn, silent, with strong heart energy; they were detached from the woodland adventures but were there should anyone need to consult.

That night I discussed the moss faery's request with my inner colleagues (something I have since learned to do on the spot). We decided I should return to the area, and we would see what was actually occurring.

The next day, as I approached the mossy hill, I was greeted by the moss faery. "Just come and see," he begged, "PLEASE!"

I stepped into the area and, following his lead, we arrived at the spot where he had been sitting the day before. It was a few moments until I could adjust to the frequency he was complaining about, but when I did, his world and his problem suddenly became very clear. As a wave of sympathy came out from me and washed over him, the moss faery visibly relaxed.

Five saplings had fallen in an orderly circle, meeting at a center point; beneath this point there was a raised knoll covered with moss. It was so neatly arranged it appeared some life form had purposely blocked the energy of this spot.

The knoll area was clean of leaves, but the saplings were too large for the moss faeries to move by themselves.

"You are right," I said. "You do have a problem. How do you want me to help?"

"If you would please just move the trees off this spot, we can do the rest ourselves," he said. There was still an air about him of hiding something.

I checked in with my inner team. I wanted to be certain I had permission to change a situation whose cause I could not see. The team said it was fine and communicated a sense of amusement to me. They let me know that while the situation did have a cause, the lesson had been learned. Given my full day's schedule and the fact that helping was a matter of mere minutes, I did not feel it necessary to investigate any further.

Being very careful not to step on the knoll and crush some of the lovely moss, I removed the saplings, then stood and looked at the site. It was a beautiful spot, regal in a faery manner with its complex pattern of roots raised above the ground, with rich green moss covering that and many holes like windows and doors into its dark rich dirt interior. "You were right," I said. "This is truly beautiful."

However, the moss faery was now completely ignoring me, focusing intently on fixing up his realm. So I continued my walk, chalking it up as an interesting experience.

It was a full moon that night, and the camp was suffused with the joy of faery spirits in harvest celebration.

The next morning I was preparing for my talk on consciousness and took a walk to sense the consciousness of the day and of the group who would attend. When I came to the moss realm that I had helped clean just the day before, my breath was taken away.

The moss hill was filled with light, top to bottom, so powerful in its joyous energy that it now far outshone the more delicate fern glen to the right. I stood and absorbed the energy and pondered what it all meant. This time it was not the moss faery but the over-lighting deva of the area who came forward and spoke with me. She explained there had been a full moon celebration here the night before. All the moss faeries of the area had come together to celebrate with dance and song the restoration of their kingdom's royal hall. I could see light emanating forth from that central knoll.

"May I enter?" I asked.

"Certainly," the response came.

So I carefully walked up the hill, avoiding the mossy areas that were living quarters for the faeries. When I reached the knoll, it was hardly recognizable from the day before. This was now once more a powerful spot, a ruling domain vibrating with earth energy. I walked up the hill a little way above this, sat down, and entered into communication.

The moss faeries came forward and thanked me for my service to their world, but the young boy moss faery was nowhere to be seen! Under the stern guidance of the deva, the moss faeries politely asked what they could do to repay me. I was surprised and a bit bewildered by this offer, because this had been my first conscious act of service to the faery world.

I heard a whisper in my ear. "Tell them you are grateful to be of service and the only payment you request is for them to teach you something more about their world so that you can be of even better service in the future."

I absorbed this instruction into my heart and then responded as cued. The faeries were delighted! We sat and communed for some time.

Then, at last, it was time for me to go. My workshop would begin soon. As we parted, I asked the woodland spirits if they had any message for humans.

"Yes," the faeries responded. "Tell them we need them. We cannot do the work without them. Humans are the arms and legs of this earth."

Lessons

On earth, we humans are truly the arms and legs of this dimension. We are stewards in the deeper sense of the word, not in the power-over manner that has occurred so often in our recent past, where humans have abused all other life forms and considered it our right to do so. It is up to us to listen to the needs of the multiple domains coexisting on earth, in various overlapping worlds, and to arbitrate a positive outcome.

If you wish to connect to the faery realm, assisting a nature spirit in distress is one way to start; you can learn one way to do this in the exercise below. At a time of need, both sides are interested in communicating and are more easily able to bridge the frequency gap between their worlds. When the nature spirits are under pressure to restore some imbalance to its "right" state of being, they go seeking help, just as we humans do.

Faeries are responsible for their domain. If something happens there, they must correct it or be held accountable by higher-ups. Some of the lower-echelon faeries can be mischievous and irresponsible, just like humans can be. If they misbehave, they may be punished by higher-ups. In this situation, the young moss faery had evidently been a bit too mischievous and had crossed the wrong elder spirit who had proceeded to demonstrate its annoyance in return. It was up to the moss faery to find a solution. This meant he had to forego his mischievous ways and be more mature in his interactions with others, or all his community would continue to suffer the loss of their central power spot!

There is no telling how long the young moss faery had been trying to solve his problem. When he first approached me, he had tried to use subterfuge and that had not worked. The next time his request had been heartfelt.

When you help a faery, their moral code states they are supposed to thank you; it is necessary to do so to maintain the balance of nature. Yet the mischievous moss faery still had not matured, and instead of thanking had studiously ignored me. He did not want to have to pay any price for my assistance, pulling a "bluff" on the human who had helped him and didn't know this code!

The leprechaun's pot of gold, which is a traditional gift requested by those who can only see the physical, was acquired by helping the leprechaun or catching him by the ankle! One of my guides had provided me with a much more suitable request than asking for outer gold. When helping another life form, requesting as a "thank you" the opportunity to learn more about their world is a much higher level of response.

In some folk tales, it is said that if a human is helped by faery spirits, the human should not thank them, for it either obligates you to them or can dissipate whatever favor they have just done for you. This is the reverse of the situation above and also derives from the old "power-over" autocratic consciousness. When someone compassionately comes forward to assist you, if you are working from an attitude of cooperation, it should continue right through the entire action, including genuine gratitude. But this is gratitude from a state of detachment, just as it should be when you interact with humans. You need to avoid being tricked by any disguised effort to make you feel obligated to the helper. This is what the young moss faery was attempting to avoid with the human who helped him.

When you have helped nature spirits and the energy has been able to once more "slot in" to its prevailing grid, what you get is a sense of returned completeness. All is once again right. It is a detached feeling. Nature is once more doing what it should be doing, so there is no more distress.

The assisting individual derives satisfaction from seeing all returned to its rightness and from the knowing inherent to our own energy field that we have assisted another living energy field to correct a problem they could not manage by themselves. This is the same sense of satisfaction our guides and guardians receive from their efforts to help us humans manage the very complex energy issues of our world. They do not ask for or expect our gratitude. All energy eventually wants to know clarity and balance, and that is one of their functions when interacting with us.

EXERCISE

Set your intent as wanting to positively communicate with nature spirits. Select a location, such as your own yard or a local preserve. This is not a time for you to bring a dog or a child with you as you want to quiet your senses to pick up the subtle frequency of the nature spirits.

When you arrive at the selected location, call your inner team to be with you. Then humbly invoke the over-lighting nature spirit of that area. You may not know whether you've reached the nature spirit, but greet him or her anyway. Express your wish to commune, to learn, and also to assist if she or he needs help. Now start on your walk. Move slowly and quietly and listen/feel/observe. Eventually you will feel a call to go in one direction or another—it might be off the beaten track—so now is the time to test your senses by following that call and seeing where it leads you. It might take you to someplace small or large.

You are being tested by the nature spirits, for you need to prove that you can assist as they require. At first it might be something as small as removing a stationary object such as a twig that is impeding the straight growth of a seedling emerging below it. In time, as you listen and participate with nature, your assistance will be requested for larger and larger projects. You can always say no to a project and if it is a large one—such as I encountered in the Princeton situation in chapter 2—you should consult with your inner team to see if they want you to take it on. They may say no, and you should feel comfortable delivering that decision to the nature spirits, who might then alter their request to meet your abilities or simply bow out of the situation and wait for some other solution.

When you have completed your assistance, sit or stand quietly. Offer gratitude to the nature spirits for permitting you to be of service. Request forgiveness from them for any of your own, or humanity's, past transgressions that occurred through ignorance. When you feel them accept this and they offer gratitude back to you and ask what they can do for you in return, request they teach you more about themselves so that you can be of greater service in the future. This is a win-win solution for everyone involved!

The Moss Faery—New Hampshire

A few years after the incident above, I was visiting with my brother on our family property in New Hampshire. I had just begun taking nature spirit photographs. One sunny August morning, the nature spirits announced that, if I wished, they would take me out and to get some photographs of faeries. I was thrilled.

Now this was a different situation from the one above. Here I was not being asked to do something, which had caused the faeries to reach out to me. I was there to take photographs of them, and these creatures are extremely shy and reserved.

I started my walk, guided by the nature spirits, and when we got to an area I had never noticed before, the nature spirits asked me to stop and take notice. The air changed, and I entered into a different frequency world than I had been in before. The energy was very light, almost weightless, in feel. The sun was suddenly very bright and sparkly, with little bright bursts of light everywhere. The dark reaches of the forest were dew-damp and rich with energy.

Right in front of me were many pine trees with beautiful gardens of moss all around their bases and the most amazing designs in their roots, just right for little faery rooms. I had the most wonderful time observing what my unseen nature guides explained was a moss faery village. I had walked past this spot many times without noticing any of this. It was a real surprise.

We walked on a bit more, and the nature spirits told me I should take photographs when and where I was told to, even if I could not see anything there. I complied and kept clicking the camera whenever I was told. But, honestly, I could not see anything myself.

I returned to the cottage and downloaded the digital images into the computer. I looked through the photos but found nothing and was quite disappointed. It was then that a nature spirit said to me, "Look at the images I tell you to stop at and the area I lead you to." I did that, and to my amazement the nature spirit was able to lead me to several areas in which a real, live, physically observable faery was present.

"How is this possible?" I asked.

The nature spirit explained that humans have too heavy a vital (emotional) consciousness to be able to see into the more refined faery world. But a camera does not have a vital consciousness. So if it is operating at the right frequency and someone tells the human where to point and shoot, the subtle life forms will be seen on the film.

This was the first time I consciously caught a nature spirit on film. I was so pleased, I wanted to go out and get more photos of the moss faeries right away! So the next day I went back to the same tree, parked myself opposite it, and started taking photographs. I don't know what I was expecting. It was quite foolish to expect that a shy moss faery would just stand there and pose as someone was invading his home!

After a little while with no success, I heard a male voice telling me with great scorn, "You are a fool!" I looked around and could see no one, so I

Figure 4.9. The moss faery's home, and the moss faery at the upper right (see circle), peeking out from under a root to see who was invading his home. This was my very first photograph of a nature spirit, and I was using a simple point and shoot camera, with not enough pixel power to facilitate a large size image.

kept invading the faery's home turf, trying to take his photo. The nature being manifested itself in a subtle physical form. It was a nature Pan.[12] He was leaning up against a tree with arms folded, shaking his head at the stupid human, telling me repeatedly, and hoping, I suppose, that his repetition would get through: "You are a fool!"

I was so new at all this, I had no idea what he was talking about. Needless to say, I got no photos.

Figure 4.10. Close-up of the moss faery.

Lessons

I try to remember my foolish behavior when I listen to other humans just learning interdimensional communication. I committed well-intentioned blunders in the process of learning, and so will you, but eventually we all become wiser.

Moss faeries live in community but on their own. They are very shy and prefer to avoid human contact. If a human discovers them, they have learned it is wisest to move on to another location. That is what happened here. I unfortunately drove the cautious moss faery away from his very pretty home!

There is a hierarchy in nature; the nature spirits exist in different levels of work parameters. There are also communities of nature spirits at different levels. The male spirit who spoke to me was a Pan spirit. He lived in the area and was observing me as I was attempting to observe the moss faery. He was not an instructive life form, such as a deva, but a being of the woods who just couldn't believe the incredible ignorance of this human!

I've walked by that mossy area over the years since, but it is still uninhabited and covered with leaves. The faery world is about peace, community, live and let live, and I had unwittingly broken their domain's rules. The faeries are able to shield themselves from humans, surrounding their domain with a frequency veil too gossamer for the grosser human energy to break through. If they so choose, they can remove the veil and we can enter; or they can thicken it to avoid detection.

Lessons

One of the themes in J.R.R. Tolkien's *Lord of the Rings* is the conscious departure of many in the faery kingdom from the cruel arena of Middle Earth. In the story, they left to exist in another more peaceful dimension. There is much truth to this in the Kali Yuga era in which we live (see pages 15–16), for we humans have done so much damage to nature in so many ways that many nature spirits withdrew, wanting nothing to do with us.

Chapter 4

When you are doing interdimensional communication, you need to stop and observe whatever field you enter into. That is because the rules are always going to be different in different realms. Each world is a merkabah—a self-contained form that has grown its own rules as it developed in its own unique manner. The experiences of these worlds may have been far different from those that have occurred on earth. These different rules mean we need to observe and act appropriately, or we can either harm something in another world or be misunderstood and rejected.

This is really no different from earth—where we need to be sensitive in our interactions to the ethics and social mores of other groups. For example, during the afternoon you may play on a rugby team where an affectionate greeting might be a big bear hug. Then later that evening, you may attend a symphony concert where an affectionate greeting might be a simple, cool nod of the head. You alter your behavior to fit the customs of the venue.

My experience with the moss faeries in Maine and then in New Hampshire taught me the importance of establishing an open, transparent relationship with the nature spirits—one of camaraderie and information exchange, not one based on "taking." Now I always pause at the entry to a nature area, thank the nature spirits for their care of the area, request permission to enter, and gently state that I would like to learn more about their world; if there is anything anyone wishes to show me, I would like to learn. Then, as I continue in, I keep my senses heightened so that I am aware when someone or something sends forth a signal out of the ordinary.

I scan an area to find a teacher or gentle leader with whom I can discuss what is occurring, and then I take any issues that arise to my inner team and ask them what to do. They always let me know whether to proceed or turn away. But I have to ask first; they are a very pragmatic and busy team, and if I do not ask, they usually will not intervene. If they say proceed, and I encounter a situation that is new to me, I am assured that either my team will know how to handle it or they will know how to locate and liaise with whomever does know. We call this "doing lunch." My team

180

goes off and has a friendly get-together with the guides and guardians of the other energies involved, they resolve the matter in a friendly way and come back to me with a resolution.

I learned from my experiences with the moss faeries in New Hampshire that I need to be more aware of the prevailing culture of the world I enter into communication with. If I had known then what I know now, I would not have caused the gentle moss faery to move from his mossy home, for his own safety and peace!

PHOTOGRAPHS

The nature photo shoot in New Hampshire was the start of my work photographing nature spirits. Although I had unwittingly distressed the moss faery, the nature spirits felt I had potential and kept working with me. By listening to where they told me to point and shoot my camera and by photographing what I could not see with my own eyes, I gradually began to participate with more awareness; as my awareness increased, I was able to see the energy they wished me to capture on film and show the public.

My inner team explained that the sheer quantity of nature spirit photographs that I would assemble would be strong evidence for the awareness and interaction possible with these life forms. This became my primary motivation for nature spirit photography. The ability to film these forms helped me develop confidence in discussing my interdimensional work. Gradually I grew in skill and eventually began taking photography classes at a community college. Don't let your current level of skill—in nature spirit communication or in photographic knowledge—affect whether or not you undertake this work; your skill will evolve!

Photographing faeries is, like other interdimensional work, done better by some people than by others. You have to be in the right frequency, or consciousness, to clearly see the faeries. If you sort of see into their realm, you may catch their energy form—what we call orbs or spheres of light. If you do see clearly—in a case where the nature spirits feel beneficent and unveil themselves—you may get images such as those shown in this chapter. The photographs of faeries that I made on this outing were a gift, but at the time, my photography skills did not match the gift!

Here are two more images of pixies from that shoot. Figure 4.11 shows a pixie looking down from his "apartment house door" in a tree trunk, and Figure 4.12 shows a pixie playing with a twig.

Figure 4.11. Pixie looking down from his "apartment window."

Figure 4.12. This shows a small pixie wearing a hat, picture center, and holding onto a twig.

THE STRANDED GNOME

Jamie and Yvonne were yogi jewelers from Canada. We were having lunch together at a yoga retreat when they asked if I had any idea what was happening in their home. They had a closet on either side of their front door, and ever since they had moved in, the smell of dirty sneakers had accosted them, sometimes in one closet, sometimes in the other, and sometimes not at all. This puzzled them greatly. At first they had thought it might be mold so they had thoroughly washed down the closets, but the smell kept intermittently returning.

"What's your take on this?" they asked me.

The moment I focused in on the issue, I saw a small gnome, huddled in the closet in fetal position, very sad, tired, and frightened.

"What's the matter?" I asked the little guy.

He looked up, and I saw dried tear lines down his dirty face. "They closed my door home, and I am stuck here," he said forlornly. "Help me!"

"What can I do?" I replied.

"Across from their front door, they built a wooded fountain area," he said. "In there is a door with another way home. But it is controlled by the trolls, and they would eat me if they found me!"

He sent me an image of some very large and frightening looking creatures; I did not blame him for not trying that route home!

"What can I do?" I repeated.

"Have the people sprinkle holy water in that area. It will clear and protect the doorway. I can then get home."

I laughed. "These are yogis. They don't believe in or have any holy water. That won't work."

"Just ask them," the gnome pleaded.

So I did. "Gnomes can sometimes smell like dirty sneakers—especially a refugee who cannot maintain his usual hygiene—and this is a good indicator of their presence," I explained to Jamie and Yvonne. "The gnome would like to leave your home and just needs your help. And," I said apologetically, "the gnome said all that was needed was to have you sprinkle some holy water in the garden. He was insisting that you had some. Is this so?"

Jamie and Yvonne looked at each other and then at me in surprise and puzzlement. "Holy water?" Jamie said to Yvonne. "Why would we have anything like that?"

I saw Yvonne inwardly scan her home. Suddenly she smiled. "Oh! Remember Suzanne went to Lourdes last year, and brought us back a vial of holy water! It's in the bookcase in your study!"

So Jamie and Yvonne promised that on their return they would do as the gnome asked to help him return home.

A few weeks later, the little gnome appeared to me while I was relaxing in my home. "Thank you," he said. "They finally remembered to sprinkle the holy water. I got inside the doorway and am hiding now. As soon as the trolls leave on an excursion, I will sneak back home."

Several days later the gnome appeared to me again. "I'm home," he said excitedly. "I made it! Thank you, thank you, thank you." And he was gone.

A few months later, I saw Jamie and Yvonne at a retreat. "So," I said, "how did it go with your gnome?" They replied quite enthusiastically that they had forgotten about the whole thing when they went home, until the dirty sneaker smell overwhelmed them in the closet. They located the holy water and sprinkled it. Very soon after, the sneaker smell disappeared and had not reappeared. All was once again well in their world!

LESSONS

Situations in which nature beings become refugees because of humans' unconscious interruption of their worlds are common in areas where the two worlds intersect, such as on a piece of land and in areas of construction. While many life forms may use a natural gateway, they are not familiar with its operating mechanisms; and once the doorway is destroyed, they do not know what to do. It is especially difficult if the portal is not a steady opening, but a timed device that opens and closes and is destroyed during an off cycle; this is one reason why in the old days people would perform a ceremony before constructing on a site, not only to locate an optimum energy site but also to get the nature spirits' permission and to alert the spirits that changes were about to occur so they could plan accordingly.

EXERCISE

Find someplace where construction is going on, or about to go on. Prepare by requesting that your inner team be with you and tell you whether you should go into this location. If they agree, prepare yourself by becoming calm and peaceful. Decide on a time of day when you will not be disturbed or the energies are quiet. Go to the site, and stand or sit quietly. Call on the nature spirits, letting them know that construction is about to begin or that it is going to continue and will be extensive. Alert them to move all the movable nature spirits to other locations and to tell the immovable spirits—the rocks, plants, and trees—to calm, center, and prepare themselves for transition to the realm of spirit. Ask if there is any way you can be of assistance. If you know the parameters of the construction and where a safe area will be, let the nature spirits know by imaging the spot to them. If the nature spirits know ahead of time, they are often able to move many to safety. Then, when construction is completed, these spirits will often move back to their old area to start repopulating.

I have often seen the results of not warning the nature spirits before the construction of large housing developments. Nature spirits are committed to their charge and will frequently go down with the charge rather than desert. However, if they know what is occurring, they may choose to withdraw and then return. In construction areas where no ceremony has been done and whole nations of nature spirits have died, there is the deathly stillness of a graveyard—even after the homes have been built. If you are living in such an area, consider reintroducing native plants and requesting the remaining refugee colonies of nature spirits who did survive to please return. I have seen this done very successfully; the remaining nature spirits, once again happy, reward the home owners with very beautiful supportive nature energy.

If you are in an area with recent large-scale construction, look about in the few remaining areas of natural vegetation. Often you will see refugee colonies there where the nature spirits are crowded together afraid and often sickly from overcrowding. Sit with the area, see what options there are to let the nature spirits move back to the land. Then go stand or sit in the refugee area and establish your intent to inform them of possibilities. When or if you feel some sort of response—believe, don't doubt—continue your efforts to connect and assist.

The Owl on Turtle Island

Trees shape themselves to the energy of their environment. For example, if a spiritual person lives in the area, a tree can assume the shape of an animal who is of special significance to the individual. This can occur even in a mature tree, who may shift consciousness and appearance when a new owner moves in. This happened at the Heartland Sanctuary, which my friends Maggie and Charlie once owned. One of their totems was an owl. About a year after they moved in, the burr oak guardian tree at the entry to their property began to manifest the shape of an owl, perched on a turtle resting in an ocean of waves—the owl on turtle island. Turtle Island is a name Native Americans have for earth, so here there was the manifestation of wise energy that could see into the darkness and was poised on earth, to offer wisdom to all and to provide protection.

Figure 4.13. Owl on turtle island. The owl's eyes and face are to the upper right; her wings are both up (the two limbs) and down (to the left, on the trunk). She sits on a turtle (head to the left, one fin hanging down), surrounded by the waves of the ocean.

LESSONS

Trees manifest the energies of their environment. As mentioned before, trees can contain several faces, or energies. In this way, they project different aspects of consciousness that they particularly want to develop and hold for their area. Trees and people interact energetically, and different areas manifest different types of energy. In my travels, I have found areas where a specific type of energy dominates and is manifested in the trees and rocks. For instance, there are areas with a strong frog energy, and the rocks and trees show that; in others there is a bird energy or a bear energy, and the trees show that. In this story, there is a family with an affinity for owl energy, and a tree with that affinity—both assisted and amplified the energy for the other.

When I see these natural images, I think of the indigenous peoples of the Pacific Northwest Coast, who are renowned for their complex totem poles—tall tree trunks with carved images of animals and humans. I like to imagine that originally, long, long ago, they may have begun by carving images to amplify the protective energies of the trees and natural surroundings with whom, as a society, they were intimately connected.

EXERCISE

In this exercise, you are going to practice sitting with a tree. It takes a while to be able to easily see tree spirit images. You need to softly adjust your eyes and your frequency. Some people can hear or feel a tree's energy before seeing it. If you have a favorite tree in your yard, go there. Or go to a peaceful park and find a tree that attracts you. Sit with it. Ask it to communicate with you. When you feel this occurring, do not doubt yourself or the process; doubt throws up an immediate barrier. Be detached and accept what is occurring. Let it happen naturally. Believe.

When the experience is over, this is the time to analyze. Once your experience with the tree is completed and you sense a disconnection, sit quietly and review inwardly what has occurred. How did the communication begin? What senses were you using? What did the space feel like? Can you replicate this experience? How would you do so—what attitude do you need, what consciousness do you need to be in or connect to? You need to start building a recipe for successful communication that works for you. This science is so young it is still experimental, and so old a practice it has gone on as long as people and trees have coexisted. Every time someone connects with a tree within our Western cultural framework, it brings this morphogenetic field, this ability, more strongly into our everyday world. It makes it easier for the next person to reach up and connect. Once you have taught yourself, start teaching those around you. Energy work is often best transmitted through identification, assimilation, and repetition.

PHOTOGRAPHS

Seeing is believing. Once you can communicate with the trees, ask them to let you photograph them so that you have proof to show others. This, too, is a cooperative process. You are requesting the tree to put more power into its manifestation of a specific energy and to hold that still so that you can photograph it. When I first started, the trees and I were so sincere about working together that often, while the rest of the environment was stationary, the tree would be blurred from its increased oscillation. So I learned to request the tree to stand still so that I could get a good image, and I also requested my energy to stay centered for it was also oscillating at a higher frequency that could affect the camera.

If you have developed a relationship with the tree, study it at different times of the day, different weather, different seasons, different angles. Sometimes it takes awhile to get just the right lighting so that the image shows well. For this reason, I now shoot in Camera Raw and use Photoshop's or Lightroom's development adjustments, which permit lightening certain parts of a photograph and darkening other parts, and increasing the image sharpness. This permits all the pertinent features to be seen, where ordinarily they might be lost in shadow or be too light. Other than that, you don't want to make adjustments. Adjustments can be felt energetically and are never as good as the natural image. Our field of interdimensional cooperation is concerned with what actually is—not with what can be artistically created from what is.

THE BALSAM WHO LOVED THE BIRCH

"I love you."

"I love you."

A masculine and a feminine voice kept calling back and forth, but I was on a lazy summer stroll along a gentle, lightly used path in the northern New Hampshire woods, and there were no people in sight.

"Would you like to see who they are?" a nature deva asked.

"Of course," I replied, and the adventure began.

To the right, on a gentle knoll that looked deep down over an ancient winding stream, stood a balsam and a birch. The deva invited me to leave the path and visit the pair. The story, she said, showed best from another angle.

As I walked up, I saw the male balsam had reached his branch arms very protectively around the female birch, in a tree embrace. They were touching each other at several points along their growth.

The connection started at the root section, where the balsam had spread out his roots surrounding and shoring up the birch on the steep hill. About three feet from the ground, the balsam had sent out a branch (looking much like a penis) that had pushed itself hard against the birch. About twenty feet above that, each tree had grown a bulbous extension, looking like lips reaching out in a kiss to each other.

The genuine love and companionship of these two was a joy to see but with a touch of sadness. The couple was in their old age now and the birch, who had a shorter lifespan, was losing its life energy. The pine tree was trying very hard to send his own life force energy to his loved one.

The deva was pleased with the love these two had developed over the years and wanted to share it with me. It was her crowning achievement, she told me.

Figure 4.14. The balsam embraces the birch as they kiss.

I enjoyed the trees' love story for some time and then started on my way. The deva invited me to return and visit her again, telling me she had more to show me. And so, over the course of my vacation, I visited this site several more times.

This deva had been experimenting, she explained on these next visits. Within her domain were a number of birches and balsams growing near each other, and they had developed a variety of relationships. Curious about this, I then checked several miles of the trail during my walk and saw very few such pairings anywhere else. It appeared to be concentrated mostly within her specific domain.

The white birches, she explained, are soft, gentle folk, supple but not very strong. The balsams are strong but somewhat stoic, stern, and withdrawn. Birches have a shorter life span than balsams. In the winter, the birches need the balsams' vigor.

The deva wanted to give the two species a chance to learn from and enhance each other, and so she had arranged for a number of pairs to grow up next to each other.

The opportunity was given. It was up to the free will of the trees to decide how to proceed.

The deva led me to see a number of the other experiments and taught me about the different energies and solutions that had occurred.

One birch was surrounded by three balsams, all of whom vied for her attention. However, she had remained the flirt throughout her life, committed to none of them, standing tall in the middle. Now this birch had died, leaving an energetic void in the middle and three lonely bachelor balsams, each growing on its own. One birch and balsam started out together, but the birch pulled away and the balsam leaned in toward her. "See, the balsam is still 'pining' away for her," the deva gently joked.

Another two (Figure 4.15.) started out together, but each began pulling away; about four feet up in growth, the birch turned at a wide angle and grew away, ignoring the energy of the balsam, choosing to grow on alone.

Then there were a birch and balsam who showed, by their trunk growth, that they had each been given several opportunities to partner with the other. There was a broken stump next to each. The birch had regrown straight. But the balsam pulled away, one shoot growing up on each side of its old stump. Instead of growing tall or reaching out to the birch, it reached

Figure 4.15. This birch tree (right) started out growing next to the balsam tree then turned and grew away.

out to aspects of itself, connecting and entwining, sending down branches into the earth that had become new root systems, growing into each other at several branch points. The result for the balsam was an intricate dance with itself, but all of the intertwined trees were small and stunted.

193

"This distorted scenario," the deva stated, "is a lesson in the problems of incestuous growth. Don't do this," the deva explained. "Reach out to others—trust—grow straight—seek new blood, new life, and new challenges. Otherwise your energy will circle back on itself and distort."

LESSONS

Devas are in charge of a specific area of land, and the nature of the deva can profoundly affect the energy of that area. Often they will undertake experiments, seeking ways to maximize the health and happiness of their land. Conversely, when there is a lot of destruction to their land through war, natural disaster, or human intervention, their own energy is depleted and their area affected. The devas are the energy of their area!

In this case, the deva was very innovative—not only a romantic but also a nature scientist. She was reformulating many of the rules of that area, including showing a human around so that her methods could be understood.

On occasion, devas will work with humans whose frequency or consciousness intersects with their own. In general, humans work on other frequency channels than the nature spirits. However, from sheer volume of repeated land consultations, some of these nature frequencies have become a part of my energy field. I am now occasionally contacted by nature spirits who are curious as to who is moving through their world at a frequency that is within their range of perception.

As consciousness is elevating in our world, heading into the Age of Spirituality, it is also affecting the ability of all life forms on earth to be aware of and communicate with one another. During the Kali Yuga, our earth descended into a solid gross physical consciousness in terms of working with existence, and all of us are now extending our awareness into other frequencies. There are now whole new options opening up for cooperation with life forms from other realms that coexist with us on earth.

PHOTOGRAPHS

Look at the plants and trees around your home. Find a commonality. Then look at the plants and trees in another area of the city, or in another park. Find a commonality. Are they different? How? How does that affect the energy of that locale?

Once you have learned to recognize the differences, start seeing the significance of this awareness. Are there areas that need your assistance? Are there areas that can assist you or others? Are there ways that you can assist nature in enhancing the natural energies for the benefits of all? Once you have determined what can be done, start documenting (with word and photo) what you have seen and done and the effects, long term, that you have assisted with. In this regard, be aware that nothing lasts forever and sometimes places you have become fond of are changed by nature or man. This is all part of the natural sequence of nature.

THE ROCK ELF AND THE MAIDEN/CRONE

One of my favorite rock scenes is a fifteen-foot-long mural in a sandstone cliff, found in a national park in Southern Illinois. Hundreds of people pass by it on an elevated walkway each day, and there is a sign nearby explaining the geological structure of this entire area. But how many ever notice this marvelous painting by the nature spirits? The area with the image is a lighter color than the darker iron-stained, moss-covered rocks that naturally frame the scene.

The mural depicts a story of unrequited love, as ancient as time itself and known throughout the universe. You can see, in Figures 4.16 and 4.17, a woman, bending over from the left, who is eternally dreaming of her lost love. Her face is simultaneously that of a young maiden, full view, and a crone with only one tooth left, side view. A bubble-line runs from her capped head to a balloon containing the image of her unrequited love, the rock elf. He is smiling at the top center, with wide cheeks, a prominent nose, and a cap on top of protruding curly hair. He appears to have left the woman for a spiritual quest; coming out of his head is a bubble with an image of clouds—or is that the canopy of snake heads that signifies the presence of Vishnu, the Hindu god in charge of preserving the world?

Beneath the woman, her right arm extends, with a bubble-line leading up, on the right, to a rear view of the elf, unclothed and muscular in all his youthful manhood. You can see his broad shoulders, tight buttocks, and muscular legs.

This is clearly too complex to be a "trick of the light." This mural clearly demonstrates that there are natural forces capable of affecting matter in a very solid way!

Figure 4.16. The rock elf and the Maiden/Crone.

Figure 4.17. Key areas circled.

LESSONS

There are children's pictures of nature spirits "painting" nature—leprechauns with a paint brush painting fall leaves or nature spirits painting sunsets. We feel these are "imaginary" representations of what is happening, but in my experience there is much truth to these images. I often go into nature and find unusual scenes that have no other explanation than a conscious interaction of spirit with matter.

When I come upon scenes such as this one, I am overwhelmed by the mysteries of nature that we humans have not yet understood. How can nature carve in the supposedly natural lines of sedimentary sandstone and iron such a detailed, coherent visual story?

Nature spirit art is there to be enjoyed by all, but you have to look for it and see with eyes of spirit. You can't rush, and it doesn't come in ten-second sound bites! For me, these phenomena are in the same category as the authentic crop circles that are being manifested right now. Some type of conscious energy is at work here. It is up to us humans to determine what is going on and to learn to work consciously with the energies involved for the benefit of us all.

It is a curious thing that in recent years, primarily with the advent of digital cameras and the availability of software programs such as Photoshop, more and more photos of life forms from other realms are beginning to surface. My team explains that some life forms exist in realms relatively close to those of earth. For humans, the barriers between the worlds often occur because we cannot surmount the vital energy barrier, which in most humans is grosser and more frenetic than that of other realms. A camera does not have the developed emotions of a human and is focused on simply recording what is occurring within its frequency range. Hence it is often able to capture a shot of a life form the human may or may not be aware of but who is within the camera's digital frequency range. Many times, people think they have a bad photo because of a streak of color going through, or an orb, or a phantom image. Sometimes these are technical issues, but sometimes they are not; they are life forms from other realms. Learning to differentiate what is captured by a camera is an evolving craft that many groups are beginning to explore, especially paranormal investigators and photographers.

Grandmother Tree

In a local park there is an old and venerable cottonwood tree—Grandmother—who is clearly at the end of her life. She is so highly regarded by the nature spirits and the other trees of the area that they have woven a web of energy around her. The roots of nearby trees circle her in protection.

Grandmother houses many contradictory energies as she weaves an energetic web of cooperation. Here is a collage of the stories around her trunk. This is a "collage of space" in which I've worked to integrate the elements.

Figure 4.18. This collage shows the key trunk and root faces of this elderly tree.

The hole to the middle left is the face of an old man licking his lips, inside a vulva-shaped hole. In the forefront is a complex series of interlocking hierarchical energies, natural opponents learning to live together: a bird head with a frog eye (left) facing an alligator, and a set of rather ominous human eyes looking on from the far right. All this is presented from the point of view of the tree, who was living in an area ripped apart by mining, restored, and then used by humans ignorant to the communicative abilities of the nature around them. The tree spirit is attempting to hold many opposing life forms together, to harmonize them.

Below is a close up of the bird head with the frog eye winking at us.

Figure 4.19. Bird head with frog eye.

The Heron, the Lizard, and the Green Faery

It was a warm and sunny September morning in a park on an island in the middle of the Fox River, reached by quaint stone bridges on either end. As part of a photography class assignment, I was studiously searching for the best angle to photograph the complex ley lines of this area.

The trees on the island leaned in keeping with the prevalent motion of the ley lines in which they were growing. The resulting tree patterns clearly crisscrossed as they spanned the island. The crossing patterns not only are very beautiful, but they effectively scrub the frequency in their energy field from one side, then the other, like the alternating pulse of a clothes washing machine, clearing and energizing all visitors who walk across these lines.

As a result, I felt cleared, relaxed, and happy as I worked. Looking for something else to photograph, I glanced at a fallen willow tree that I had been photographing over the past year. Willow trees are gentle folk, very soothing emotionally, and old willow trees have wonderfully gnarled roots whose patterns are intriguing. There was some special energy connected to this particular willow that I could not quite see, and it drew me back repeatedly to fathom its secret. Suddenly a faery voice spoke in my ear. "All right, go on over. We will provide you with the definitive photograph of this tree!"

Leisurely, enjoying the warm sun, I strolled over to stand in front of the beautiful willow on the very edge of the river. It had split and fallen over many years before. Part of it was dead, and the rest whirled about in fascinating patterns. It was a favorite seat for many a walker and many an audience member of the local concerts in the park.

The faery energy came forward, and I was able to see more profoundly than before. "What do you see?" she prodded.

I looked carefully and saw a bird's head. I snapped several pictures.

"Is that it?" the faery asked, in a teasing voice.

"I guess so, thank you," I responded politely.

"Why don't you walk around to the other side of the tree?" the faery teased.

I did, and as I had done many times before, enjoyed looking at the gnarly patterns of the living trunk, with the gnarly, split-off, grey section of dead trunk beside it.

"What do you see?" the faery asked again.

"Beautiful wood patterns," I responded.

"Look again," the faery said. There was a slight adjustment in the energy of that space, and in myself, and suddenly—like veils being removed from my eyes—I could see deeper into the energy than before. And there before me, so clear that I could not believe I had never seen it before, was a magnificent blue heron in profile, its eye and slightly open beak looking to the right, its wing and chest to the left!

"Is that all?" the faery asked.

"Yes?" I responded with a question.

"Look again, out farther," the faery said, becoming somber as she entered into a teaching mode.

Suddenly, in the dead trunk to my right, I saw the wood image of a lizard, fully stretched out and looking at the heron. I was stunned. What a sight—two natural enemies fixed in place next to each other, associating together year after year.

"What does it mean?" the faery asked.

This time I simply waited for her to tell me.

"In this area, this sacred Fox River area, we nature spirits have worked hard to bring together natural enemies to peacefully coexist."

I thought back to earlier in the day when I had been visiting another Fox River park. There, too, I'd seen images of natural enemies coexisting in trees and rocks. Then my thoughts flew to St. Charles, one town up the river, where a statue honors the Potawatomie people who held the land sacred. When they were forced out by white settlers, the story goes, they peacefully left behind a blessing instead of a curse, asking only that the white man love and care for the peaceful land as their tribe once had.

There was, indeed, a pattern throughout the valley, and now I was learning this was an intentional act by the nature spirits of the area.

The faery had me take several photographs of the willow tree and, when I digitally processed them, I discovered a distinctive green orb sitting on the willow trunk. I had caught the faery's energy on camera as well!

Figure 4.20. The heron is on the upper trunk, looking right; the lizard is on the dead root to the lower right; the green faery shows as an orb on the trunk to the upper right.

A few nights later, this faery appeared to me during the night, waking me. After announcing that she was the Green Faery, she said, "From now on, I will work with you."

And she has been faithful in her promise. From that time on, when I'm on a photographic outing that is focused on nature spirits, I'll suddenly feel "in the zone"—that special place where all is in harmony and I feel one with nature. It is at this time that I get my best photographs. When I process them, I sometimes discover she has shown up in one of the first of my series of really, really good shots. She often appears as a green orb or a series of green orbs interconnected and descending in size, as she brings down into the physical range various subtle frequencies for me to successfully photograph.

With her assistance, my nature spirit photography has advanced significantly, and I am now able to show very complex stories that astound me in their richness of content.

Lessons

The Green Faery is a nature spirit energy, sometimes called a deva and sometimes an earth angel, who exists throughout the earth consciousness. She is a mother-like energy who enlists cooperation from all within her domain, or family—the earth as a whole—much like an archangel such as Michael. Both can appear wherever needed or called upon. Each has the ability to consciously contact humans they wish to interact with, inform, and inspire. The Green Faery chose to reveal herself to me after I had been consciously working to demonstrate the aliveness of nature for some nine years. Since the first time, she often manifests in photographs when I am in the "zone" and really in tune with the nature energies around me.

During a nature spirit photography workshop held at one of my favorite parks one summer, there were a number of very promising nature spirit photographers in the group. As we walked to an area I wanted them to photograph, I was inwardly intensely invoking the Green Faery to help these people learn how to properly connect. When we arrived in the nature vortex area, I explained to the workshop attendees the principles of how the energy worked there and then had them wander about and take photographs. Several weeks later, several of the women who proved especially good at this art sent me photographs they had taken in various parts of the vortex, each with a brilliant green orb highly visible! These women have since grown considerably in their abilities to photograph nature spirit energy and have had the green orb appear in a number of their photos. In the one shown here, the Green Faery moved into manifestation on the physical plane so fast that, in the click of a shutter, her right side is slightly squished from her motion. I am in the far background, where I have been invoking her to appear as I guide the participants to perceive and be able to photograph nature—each according to their own orientation. The Green Faery was coming forward to provide this.

Figure 4.21. Photographers in vortex, with Green Faery orb to top right.

The Green Faery is near the top of the hierarchy of nature energies that govern earth; her function is communication—connecting nature to humans.

There is a very broad hierarchy of capacity in the faery world. At the lower levels, there are fairies for each flower, and the fairy lives and dies with the plant. At a higher level, there are faeries associated with place, such as residents of a glen. Some are solitaries, and some live in community. If circumstances weaken their area of responsibility, the faery is weakened as well.

Some nature spirits serve as guardians for plants, just as some angels serve as guardians for people. This is especially true when the tree (or rock or nature area) has a profound role to play in the energy of that area or of earth. Sometimes the tree or rock is serving as a place holder, or linchpin, in a larger energy grid. This tree or rock will then have very powerful forces working through it to sustain a specific field of energy.

Devas are a higher order of intelligence than nature spirits. Nature devas are life forms who oversee different domains within nature. Devas are in charge of an area that may include nature spirits, wildlife, plants, and humans passing through or residing there. They have a hierarchy as well, with devas in charge of groups of devas.

Nature devas are excellent colleagues to work with, and they can teach you about the workings of their domain. You have to be benign or positive in your objectives, or of use to them in some way, or they will not let you know their secrets. Humans have the capacity to affect physical matter very rapidly, which is valuable to a deva but also potentially detrimental.

Each nature deva is in charge of his or her own domain. It is the devas' responsibility to see that all within their domain grows, learns, evolves, and succeeds. They work with many subgroups of life forms and are themselves part of ever-increasing-in-size energy families. Humans are the same, only we often do not recognize this. We are each part of ever-increasing-in-size communities, from the cells of our body up to our soul families and to source itself. We are an aspect of each of these groups. We can be unconscious of these interconnections, or we can become conscious and thus become even more effective in our own work and lives. Becoming conscious is becoming transformed and taking an aware part in the transformation process.

EPILOGUE

WHAT HAPPENS NEXT?

You have now read many stories about incidents involving humans and life forms from other dimensions. The possibilities for interaction between humans and varied frequencies in our universe are vast. As you can see, learning to communicate with other life forms holds many benefits for our world, and for each of us.

You are the physical result of eons of consciousness choosing willingly to descend from the unmanifest source into solid form. You have in the make-up of your own specific consciousness the "cellular" knowledge of all these planes; you simply need to remember to keep extending the limits of your consciousness to be aware of who you are and where you have been.

As has been shown throughout these stories, you can only see and transform what you can imagine to exist. That's why you have an inner team—one made up of beings who can see into other planes of reality, and who have the inner contacts to acquire information about various situations you will be encountering. They can teach you and prepare you to work with them as their equal.

You also need assistance from experts in our own third dimension, for they know how energy descends in other ways. I recommend you seriously explore various modalities now being practiced, such as DNA reactivation, Reiki, yoga, meditation, and so on. You will have to be discerning, for some teachers and disciplines are more effective and more aligned with your energy than others.

To assist you in your development, I and my colleagues have established many educational avenues. If you feel so moved, please visit our website, crystal-life.com! There you will find a great deal of free information, downloads, referrals, contests, and products that encourage a healthy interdimensional lifestyle. If you are near Geneva, Illinois, please visit our store. Both there and at our website, you'll find a variety of natural crystals, gemstones, and products using sacred geometry and resonant substances, and also a large gallery with color photographs of nature spirits. Via our YouTube videos, crystal-life.com/blog, and Facebook pages, you can meet other people interested in this topic and also post your questions for this community.

EXERCISE

In this final exercise, get a pencil and paper and sit down quietly. Assess all that you have read. What has particularly resonated with you? These are probably areas for which you have a natural affinity, or a need to solve. Make a list of these areas, what you feel you should do, and how you will proceed. Make a time plan and determine what result or experience will signify that you have affected, corrected, and/or mastered the situation. Don't worry if it seems absurd that you could ever master this discipline. If you put forth the intent, specify it in detail, ask for assistance, and do your part by practicing the art—you will succeed!

The forces at work in our world today are looking for receptive people with initiative, courage, determination, and persistence. Once you demonstrate that you want to learn and will work to actualize this ability, you will receive support. Be open to this support, which may come in ways you do not expect.

And one final word of caution—make sure that you ask for this change to come smoothly, safely, and gently. The universe is very literal, and if you ask for immediate transformation, you might get it—and possibly along with it a very strong upheaval in your personal life!

PHOTOGRAPHS

If you wish to pursue a visual recording of your work, treat yourself to a decent digital camera. If you wish to photograph orbs, use a lower-end point-and-shoot or a cell phone camera, as, currently, these usually do not have infrared correction; many of the orbs who are photographed at happy events apparently exist in the infrared frequency. Unfortunately, images taken with these cameras do not blow up well; they are very grainy. If you wish to photograph life form images found in trees and rocks, a better camera with good pixel resolution is useful, as the images are sharper and can be enlarged. These higher-end cameras can capture orbs whose energy exists at a higher frequency, such as devic, spiritual, and angelic energies.

Use a good photo editing program to work with your photos on the computer. Always save the original photo untouched. Make a duplicate copy and work on that; over time and with technological advances, you may wish to go back to the original and work with it more effectively. Always save the photograph you are working on in a nondestructive format such as a .tiff or a .psd. Do not use .jpg, which is how most photographs come into a camera. You should convert a .jpg to a .tiff or .psd when you begin work with it. Otherwise, every time you save in .jpg format, the photograph degenerates; pixels lost are unrecoverable. It is best to work in raw format if you can, for this has the broadest pixel base and you can most readily adjust the exposure and contrast; save your photos as a .tiff or .psd or whatever is the fullest way possible in your photographic program. Save the photograph in a large resolution, between 240 and 400 pixels, and in a large image size, such as 8x12 or 8x10. When you reduce to print, save that reduction as another image; moving back and forth in size causes you to lose pixels/clarity.

Have fun! And if you care to share your images with others, drop by crystal-life.com/blog, fill out the photographic form, and send it in! While you're there, drop by the interdimensional cooperation rooms, and see what others have been capturing on film as well!

Notes

1. According to Wikipedia: "In the New Testament, references to Melchizedek appear only in the Epistle to the Hebrews (later first century AD), though these are extensive (Hebrews 5:6, 10; 6:20; 7:1, 10, 11, 15, 17, 21). Jesus Christ is there identified as a priest forever in the order of Melchizedek quoting from Ps. 110:4."

2. This is a very simple explanation of the energetic principles of a merkabah, for the purposes of this book. For a full discussion of the technicalities of a merkabah, see *We Are Not Alone: A Complete Guide to Interdimensional Cooperation* by Atala Dorothy Toy (Weiser Books, San Francisco, CA, 2009). An excellent book on the sacred science of the merkabah, written by a metaphysical physicist, is: *The Ancient Secret of the Flower of Life*, Volume I by Drunvalo Melchizedek (Light Technology Publishing, Flagstaff, AZ, 1998).

3. According to this understanding, many life forms generally considered by Western culture as "objects" are actually "life forms" and deserving of being referred to as "who" not as "that." You may observe this differing type of reference throughout this book.

4. Burls, burrs, and tree growths. "Burr" is the English version of this term; "burl" is the American version. You will see both terms used here, depending upon generic use in America for that tree. For instance, when referring to the American redwood, the term is "burl." But when referring to the Midwest burr oak—so-named by English settlers for its many burrs—the term is "burr." There is much discussion as to what causes a burr/burl. Some feel it is an infestation, a result of an insect bite, a virus, or dormant limb buds. Some burr growths are not caused by these factors, and experts freely admit they don't understand the process of their creation. Tree images can start many ways but they develop into living expressions of the tree's energy as it works to "speak its truth." These complex growths are usually found on older trees—ones who have experienced a lot in their many dozens or hundreds of years of life—and who are expressing their views of their experiences in their own bodies.

5. As consciousness descends from the state of total unity, or oneness, it begins to differentiate itself into what we call time and space. These distinctions get

more complex as energy descends from light to liquid light to solid form. Multiple times and spaces coexist at any specific location. When the energy forms holding these different dimensions are weakened or breeched, different dimensions can bleed over into each other. Some situations I work with occur at these locations. Solutions include helping the life forms return to their own worlds and then repairing the light grid that was breeched at that point.

6. A holding field is a space that has been energetically fenced in by someone. The purpose of the fencing is to protect or isolate what is inside the field from what is outside the field. The field holds the energy in place so that it can be worked with in some fashion. It can be done by conscious will power, which could dissipate when a person's attention is diverted, or it can be anchored in objects and these can hold an energy in a specific area. Energy work sometimes involved disassembling holding fields unconsciously in place through some intense activity that occurred within it, such as a death or a battle.

7. Suspending something in time/space is another way of holding an object large or small that will be worked with at another time. Humans do that at a simple level—"I'll deal with that issue tomorrow" and they put the matter aside until the next day. Adepts in energy can establish locations where they consciously energetically place objects to work with at a future time—sort of like a cosmic locker. They can then energetically "lock the door" so the objects cannot be found by others.

8. This is a remarkable achievement that shows the ability of the medicine man, and thus his heritage, to work with natural forces. This was this medicine man's cosmic hiding place for this issue. Visually, if you can imagine consciousness as layers of frequency that go out from an object—something like those nested Russian matryoshka dolls, or like taking a compass and drawing larger and larger circles around the same central point, or like drawing one straight line above another above another—you can see the concept. The medicine man went to that soft mobile space between two objects or frequencies, placed the village there, and then, as though the space was a piece of putty, stretched and folded the space around the village. This kept the village suspended in time and space until it was retrieved. The medicine man tied the village in place with energetic lines placed about his medicine circle. For movie buffs a visual image would be the 1954 film *Brigadoon*, which is about a Scottish village that is suspended in time, returning one day every hundred years.

9. Occultists will sometimes use a "power over" procedure in which they bind another life form to control it—think of Dobby the house elf in the Harry Potter series. This is imposing one life form's will over another life form and is a lower level of working with energy than that of a person using the spiritual

energy of love to transform a situation for the benefit of all. Marty's approach was a spiritual one.

10. Dr. Ibrahim Karim is an architect based in Cairo, Egypt. He has done extensive research on how form affects energy, which he has formulated into a discipline he calls BioGeometry®. He has used this discipline to balance architectural spaces, land, and the human energy field. His website describes his work thus: "We are all dynamic living energy systems, existing in the sea of energy vibrations that is our world. Our vital energy systems are in constant interaction with each other and with our environment, exchanging energy effects on all levels. These energy effects can be grouped or categorized in a qualitative scale according to their resonant and harmonic effects on biological energy systems. Based on a Physics of Quality, the revolutionary science of BioGeometry uses the subtle energy principles of geometric form to introduce natural balance to the different energy-qualities found in any living system." (www.biogeometry.com/english/)

11. The present moment is a specific frequency. By shifting your frequency, you can shift your location in the time/space continuum. Those working with higher consciousness, from medicine people to spiritual masters, are aware of this and use the knowledge in their work to affect matter.

12. A Pan is a nature spirit with the torso of a man and the legs of a goat. Such spirits are often depicted leaning against a tree and playing Pan pipes—a form of a flute. They are carefree spirits who interact with humans on the emotional level and who, unlike faeries and devas, do not have any responsibilities for the area they live in.

Index

Bold indicates figures.

3Ms, 6–7, 9, 16, 91, 218

A

Academy of Future Science, 6

affinities, 24

Age of Spirituality, 194

alpha trees, 137–40, **139, 140,** 153

altars, 159, 163, **163, 164**

American Society of Dowsers, 76

ancestors, 13

Ancient Secret of the Flower of Life, The (Melchizedek), 7, 211

angel(s), 13, 33–34

artists, 80

ascended masters, 13

aura (life force energy), 16

Aurobindo, Sri, 15

automatic writing, 87

B

Bachler, Käthe, 133–34

Bailey, Alice, 23

balance

    BioGeometry® and, 213

    in energy fields, 9

balsam, 190–94, **191, 193**

base location

    in time/space portals, 120, **120,** 124

Besant, Annie, 23

bhakti (devotional) yoga, 10

BioGeometry®, 104, 121, 213

birch, 190–94, **191, 193**

Blavatsky, Madame, 3, 88, **88**

blessing, 202

blog, 168

Blue Papaya youth group, 28, 30, 53, 90

blue-grey intermediate zone, 22, 34–35, 47, 49

    time in, 45

body portal, 137, **140**

bog orb, 130–32, **131**

Book of Knowledge: the Keys of Enoch®, The (Hurtak), 7
Bosch, Hieronymous, 80
break offs, 22
briar bushes, 47, 147–49
Brigadoon (film), 212
burr oak, **19**
burrs and burls, **19**, 82, 143, 175, 211

C
Cain, Marty, 76–77
cameras, 29–30, 209
cat, ghost, 49–50
cell phone towers, 110
ceramic EMF clearing devices, 109
channeling, 85–86, 89
chanting, 26
children, advanced perception in, 28, 53, 90
churches, energy in, 133–35
clearing
  process of, 52–53
  water, 152
collages, 153–55, **154, 155**, 198, **199**, 200, **200**
communication. *See also* interdimensional communication
  blocked, 80–83
  Green Faery and, 205–6
  with nature spirits, 174–75

consciousness
  cellular knowledge and, 207
  descended from unity, 211–12
  evolving, 156
  intention and, 44
  merkabah and, 7
  of life forms, 103
  transformation and, 206
construction, 132–34, 185–86
cooperation. *See* interdimensional communication
cottonwood trees, 137–40
crone, 195–96, **196, 197**
crop circles, 198
Crystal children, 53, 90
Crystal Life Technology, 28, 35, 53
  blog of, 168
  website of, 82, 196, 208

D
dark forces, 84
death
  angel of, 33–34
  preparing for, 44–45
  transition to, 34–35
Delphi oracle, 86–87
detonations, 132–33
devas
  Green Faery as, 204
  guiding tree growth, 190–94
  house, 110–11, 114–15
  nature, 21–22, 206
  time/space portals and, 121–22

digital cameras
nature spirit art and, 198
selecting, 29, 209
dimensions
boundaries between, 13
communication through, 70–71
intersecting, 102–4
of merkabahs, 11
of nature spirits, 20
parallel, 24
rules of, 150–52
directions, cardinal, 92
divine light, 10
Djwhal Khul, 23
Dobby (house elf in Harry Potter
series), 212
doors (portals)
in transition to death, 38–39
dowsers and dowsing, 14, 76, 133,
166
drakon, **74**

E
ears, ringing in, 81
earth angel, 204
earth as merkabah, 11
Earth Deva, 21
earth energy, 138
Earth Radiation (Bachler),
133–34
east, 92
electromagnetic fields (EMF)
effects of, 98–102, 106–9

mitigation of, 110–11
pine trees and, 141–42, 145–46
elves, 21
Emoto, Masaru, 152
energy and energies
artists and, 80
aura and, 16
blocked, 81
competing, 141
devas and, 194–95
earth or land, 78–79, 138
fields, 11
grid, 38
in churches, 133–35
merkabah as ball of, 7–10
negative, 47, 142–43
nodes, 151
of Ganesh, 151–52
of stones, 159–63, **160, 161,
162, 164**
positive and negative, 147–48,
148–49
practitioners, 39–40, 43–44, 60
shaping trees, 186–87, **187,** 188
travel of, 103
evergreens, 111
evolution
of consciousness, 156
of thought forms, 23
variations in, 9
exercises
on affinities, 208–9
on communication, 174–75

on guardians of place, 104–6

on house devas, 114–15

on intention, 91–94

on invocations, 25–27

on land energies, 72, 79–80

on nature spirits and
   construction, 185–86

on observation, 156

on power lines and EMF fields,
   111

on seeking answers, 165–66

on sinkholes, 146

on transition to death, 34–35,
   39, 44–45

on trees and tree spirits, 123–
   24, 146, 188–89

on vortexes, 134–35

F

Facebook, 28

faery realm, 21, 71, 104, 205–6

fairies

   fern, 168

   moss, 168–72

   punishment of, 135–37

   term, 21–22

flower of life, 7–8

folds in time, 57–69

forgiveness, 51–52

France, Melanie J., 17

free will, 55, 59, 84–85

frequencies, 20, 24

   infrared, 29, 209

G

Ganesh, 151–52

geopathic fields, 75

ghost(s)

   cat, 49–50

   choices of, 37–38

   communicating with, 43–44

   dish-washing, 39–43

   final tasks of, 43

   forgiveness and, 51–52

   in haunted hotel, 53–55

   links to people and places, 46,
      49, 53–56

   Mafioso, 45–48

   novena and, 50–53

   term, 22

   time and, 44

Gilbert, Robert, 121

gnomes, 21, 183–85

God the Father, 26

God the Mother, 26

Goya, Francisco, 80

gratitude, 79, 173

Green Faery orbs, 154, 202–5

grids

   energy, 11, 103

   ley lines and, 14

   universe as, 38

guardians of place

   as thought forms, 22–23

   communicating with, 104–6,
      206

   ghosts as, 55–56

Native American, 98–102
New Hampshire spring, 73–78
guides, spirit, 80–83

H
haric line, 105
harmony, 43
Harry Potter series, 212
heart portal, 137–38, **138, 139**
Heartland Sanctuary, 187
Herman, Ronna, 89
higher self, 13, 89
Hinduism, 15–16
holding field/holding space, 26,
    58, 153–55, 212. *See also* setting
    space
holiness, 28–29
holy water, 184
horses, 106–9
hotel, haunted, 53–55
houses, sale of, 50–52, 110–15
human beings
    as stewards on earth plane, 20,
        172–74
    channels of energy in, 105
    devas and, 194
Hurtak, J. J., 6

I
Indigo children, 53, 90
infrared, in photography, 29, 209
inner team. *See also* roundtable of
    guides; spirit guides

assistance from, 207
connecting with, 13, 84–85,
    91–94
Native American village and,
    58
insanity, 12–13, 71
Institute for the Study of
    Interdimensional Cooperation
    (ISIC), 28
intention, 44, 85, 91–94
interaction of humans with nature
    spirits, 20–22
interconnectedness, 152
interdimensional communication
    blocked, 80–83
    nature of, 85–87, 89
    process of, 9–10, 24–25
    rules for, 180
    undertaking, 12–13, 70–71,
        174–75
interworld communication.
    See interdimensional
    communication

J
Jesus Christ, 6, 34, 211

K
Kali Yuga, 15–16, 87, 179, 194
Kamadon, Alton, 7
Karim, Ibrahim, 104, 213
King, Stephen, 54, 89
Kuthumi, 88, **88**

L

land energies

differences between locales and, 195

in Native American village, 57–69

surveying, 78–79

Leadbeater, C. W., 23

leprechauns, 173

ley lines

clearing, 41

description of, 14–15

personal, 81

teaching, 150–52

trees and, 201

life force energy (aura), 16

life forms, 12, 20, 211

light

as path for energy, 103

in photographs, 189–90

invocation of, 26

merkabah as, 11

transition to, 34–35

truth, 34

universe as grid of, 38

Lightroom (software), 30, 189

Lord of the Rings (Tolkien), 179

M

Mafioso ghost, 45–48

magnolia trees, 117–25, **119, 120**

maiden, 195–96, **196, 197**

mandala, 8

mantra, 44

manufactured objects, 28–29

Masons, 96–98, 121

Mayan calendar, 16

medicine man, 30, 60–61, **64, 65, 66,** 212

medicine wheel, 83

Melchizedek, 5–7, 13, 91, 211

Melchizedek, Drunvalo, 7, 211

merkabahs (balls of energy)

characteristics of, 7–11

during invocation, 26

humans as, 133

rules in each, 180

Metatron, Archangel, 5–6, 91

Michael, Archangel, 6, 25, 89

mind portal, 137, **140**

morphogenetic web, 97–98, 152, 189

Morya, 88, **88**

moss faeries, 168–72, 175–77, **177**

motivations, 85

N

Native Americans

cooperation and, 141

medicine people of, 75

totem poles and, 188

village of, 57–69, **62, 63**

nature spirits

characteristics of, 20–22

construction and, 185–86

open relationship with, 180

orbs and, 16

photographing, 29, 90–91, 177, **177, 178**

nature, answers from, 165–66

Navajo time cycles, 16

negative energy, 47–48, 58, 142–43, **144,** 145, 147–48

Night Dreams (Goya), 80

nodes, 15, 42–43, 151

north, energetic, 92

Nostradamus, 16

novena, 50–53

O

observation, 7, 18

oracle at Delphi, 86–87

orbs

    bog, 130–132, **131**

    Green Faery, 154

    photographing, 17, **17,** 209

    term, 16–17

owl, 186–87

P

Padula, Lanette, 18

Pan, 177, 179, 213

photographs and photography

    collages, 153–55, **154, 155,** 198, **199,** 200, **200**

Green Faery and, 202–5, **203, 205**

of ghosts, 35–36

of interdimensional life forms, 27–31

of land energies, 195

of nature spirits, 72–73, 90–91, 181–82

of pixies, **182, 183**

of rock images, 166–68

of spirit guides, 94–96

of trees, 123–24, 189–90

of vortexes, 149

patience and, 156–57

techniques in, 30–31, 209

Photoshop (software), 30, 189

Physics of Quality, 213

pine trees, 141–43, **144,** 145–46

pixies, 182, **182, 183**

plasma, 11, 16

polarity in merkabah, 8

portals. *See also* time/space portals; vortexes

    as gateways, 15, 103

    as timed devices, 185

    cottonwood trees and, 137–40, **138, 139, 140**

    effects on humans of, 129–30

    frequencies of, 137–40

    in transition to death, 38–39

Potawatomi peoples, 141, 202

"power over" procedure, 212–13

protection by thought forms, 75

Q
Quaker tradition, 10

R
Rainbow children, 53, 90
Roberts, Jane, 89
rock elf, 195–96, **196, 197**
rock images, 165
rock spirits, 159-63, **160, 161, 162**
roundtable of guides, 80–83,
    92–94. *See also* inner team;
    spirit guides

S
sacred geometry, 26
sacred sites, 75
Satya Yuga (Golden Age of
    Spirituality), 15
satyr, **74**
schizophrenics, 71
Second Coming of Christ, 16
Sedona, 165
self-awareness, 9, 15
sensitives, 86, 90
Seth material, 89
setting space, 26, 81. *See also*
    holding field/holding space
Shining, The (King), 54
sinkholes, 141–146
Slim Spurling agricultural
    harmonizer, 109

soul family, 13, 68
south, 92
spin of merkabah, 11
spirit guides, 92–96. *See also* inner
    team; roundtable of guides
spirits of place, 22–23, 104–6,
    111–12
St. Germain, 88, **88**
St. Michael line, 14, **14**
stabilizing objects
    in time/space portals, 120–21,
    124
Stanley Effect, 54
Stanley Hotel, 53–55
Star of David, 8
star tetrahedron, 8–9
stewardship, 172–74
sushumna, 105

T
teaching ley lines, 150–52
Theosophical Society, 4–5, 23, 88
thought forms
    image of, 30–31
    of medicine man, **66, 67,** 75
    term, 22–23
Thought Forms (Besant and
    Leadbeater), 23
time
    as cyclical, 15
    folds in, 57–69
    movement through, 24–25
    suspended in, 67

time/space
  coexistence in, 211–12
  fields, 103
time/space portals. *See also*
  portals; vortexes
  at Swarthmore College, 117–22,
    121, 122
  elements of, **119, 120,** 120–21,
    124
Tolkien, J. R. R., 179
totem poles, 188
totems
  bear, **18, 19**
  in inner team, 13
  photographing, 94–95, **95**
Toy, Atala Dorothy, 7, 24, 211,
  217–19
transition to death, 34–35
Treatise on Cosmic Fire, A (Bailey
  and Djwhal Khul), 23
tree spirits, 170, 188–89
trees
  burrs and burls on, 211
  electronic pollution and,
    106–7
  holding space, 153–55
  ley lines and, 201
  local earth energy of, 145
  meridians of, 141–43, **144**
  relationships between, 190–94,
    191, 193
  shaping to energies, 186–87,
    187, 188

spirit art and, 198, **199,** 200, **200**
triangle, 8
trolls, 21, 184
Turtle Island, 186–87, **187**

U
unity, 211
universe
  as alive and conscious, 28–29,
    71
  as light grid, 38
  as merkabah, 9

V
vesica pisces, 118, **119, 120,** 121,
  124
vortexes. *See also* portals; time/
  space portals
  around tree, 124–29, **126, 127,
    128, 129**
  as intersecting dimensions, 15,
    102–4
  clearing, 41
  in Native American village, 58
  positive and negative, 100,
    147–49
  unstable, 125–29, **126, 127,
    128, 129**

W
water
  clearing, 152
  electrical energy and, 108–9

We Are Not Alone: A Complete Guide to Interdimensional Cooperation (Toy), 7, 24, 211, 218
west, 92
White Mountains, 165

will imposed on others, 212–13
willow trees, 201

Y

yin/yang circle, 118

About the Author

Atala Dorothy Perry Toy was brought up as a Philadelphia Quaker, a Christian tradition with several sects that is united by one major tenet: there is that of God in every human being, it is known as the inner light, and we each have direct connection to that source of all knowledge, all awareness, all existence. We do not need an intermediary to connect to source; we contain this source inside ourselves.

Atala was educated at Swarthmore College, a Quaker-founded school with the highest level of academic distinction. It emphasizes research, accountability, accuracy, and has many radical professors who, during her time there, challenged the students with such "new" Western societal concepts as the cyclical nature of time and energy and the equality of all life forms who should be respected for their individual uniqueness.

Atala's first job after college was handling humanities publicity for the Massachusetts Institute of Technology. She married, was fortunate to be a stay-at-home mom, and raised two amazing sons, Steven Toy and Brian Toy. She and her family lived in an in-city yoga ashram environment where Atala learned to channel the energy to run twenty-four hour races and to be comfortable in an environment in which the very real presence of gods and goddesses, and communication with those in other worlds, was accepted as the norm. After her children were grown and she was on her own, she served as a staff member in the public relations department of the United Nations Development Programme. While at UNDP, she suffered a bout of electromagnetically-based environmental illness so severe the doctors warned her she would die if she didn't change something. She shifted from observing and doing for others to paying attention to herself.

She learned to read energy and to communicate with spirit to make concrete, effective changes, first in her own health, and then for others.

At this time, Atala began working with a team of inner guides led by a trio known as the 3Ms: Archangels Metatron, Melchizedek, and Michael. They sometimes work with solitary practitioners, teaching how to observe energy in a different way from the current societal norm, and they do so with much good humor. They insist on their human colleagues recognizing and accepting the fact that there is no superior or inferior in this partnership. We are all equals, colleagues around an inner roundtable, each with an important role and an equal say in what is to occur for our team.

These inner colleagues requested that Atala set out on her own and form a company, Crystal Life Technology, Inc. (crystal-life.com), to provide the public with subtle energy tools and information. They insisted on "Technology" being part of the name because, they said, work with crystals and crystalline energy fields was a bona fide technology and would soon become recognized as such. These inner colleagues helped Atala create, locate, and assemble energetic tools, explaining to her their energetic functions.

This inner team eventually requested that Atala write down her experiences. The radical changes she was experiencing and her struggle to comprehend their "why" meant she was able to understand "normal" perception and explain to "normal" people how to move into extended perception.

Atala spent nine years traveling the country on the metaphysical circuit, showing her products and teaching classes, and she was asked by the Melchizedeks during that time to move from the East Coast to the Midwest—to the heartland of America. She did so, settling down and eventually opening a store.

Earlier in her career, Atala had published a book, *Explorations in Consciousness*, which explored consciousness from a Western yogic viewpoint. After she settled in the Midwest and opened a store, she published a second book, *We Are Not Alone: A Complete Guide to Interdimensional*

Cooperation, which explored consciousness from a more radical departure in time/space and focused on spiritual-scientific concepts.

Next, the Melchizedeks requested that Atala photograph nature spirits. Although she told them she was not a photographer, they responded: "No problem, just point and shoot where we tell you, we'll do the rest." They explained that telling people about spirits was one thing, but being able to repeatedly photograph them provides the type of visual proof that society currently needs. One or two photographs could be an "accident" or "freak" experience; an entire collection of these images would provide more solid proof. Atala eventually began studying photography so that she could take better photographs of the life forms she was able to visually record. She personally favors nature spirits, and so these images currently predominate in her photographic collection.

This book focuses on one area of Atala's interdimensional experiences to date, and those of her clients: the realm of nature spirits and life forms close to our own.

Quest Books

encourages open-minded inquiry into
world religions, philosophy, science, and the arts
in order to understand the wisdom of the ages,
respect the unity of all life, and help people explore
individual spiritual self-transformation.

Its publications are generously supported by
The Kern Foundation,
a trust committed to Theosophical education.

Quest Books is the imprint of
the Theosophical Publishing House,
a division of the Theosophical Society in America.
For information about programs, literature,
on-line study, membership benefits, and international centers,
see www.theosophical.org
or call 800-669-1571 or (outside the U.S.) 630-668-1571.

Related Quest Titles

The Boundless Circle: Caring for Creatures and Creation,
by Michael W. Fox

Earth Energies, by Serge King

Fairies at Work and Play, by Geoffrey Hodson

Gaia's Hidden Life, by Shirley Nicholson, with Brenda Rosen

The Real World of Fairies, by Dora van Gelder Kunz

Thought Forms, by Annie Besant,
with C. W. Leadbeater

To order books or a complete Quest catalog,
call 800-669-9425 or (outside the U.S.) 630-665-0130.

More Praise for Atala Dorothy Toy's

Nature Spirits, Spirit Guides, and Ghosts

"Atala Dorothy Toy takes amazing photographs that explore myriad ways nature and people are interconnected. With her characteristic warmth and wisdom, she inspires others' exploration. Urging readers to sit and observe, reach out in peace, and work in community, she offers powerful lessons and practical exercises that nurture interdimensional photographers. I'm inspired!"

—Donna Latham, author of *Ghosts of the Fox River Valley*
and *Ghosts of Interstate 90*

"With deep respect for Atala's vision, I recommend her new book. The stories and photographs and her insights into 'feeling' and communicating with interdimensional beings will expand and bring balance to the way we view 'reality.'"

—Francene Hart, visionary artist

"Atala is a master teacher and lover of all forms of life. You are in good hands for learning how to communicate with all the creatures in our world, seen and unseen. So settle down for a good read and be open to an amazing adventure into Nature."

—Marty Cain, MA, MFA, labyrinth builder;
vice president of the American Society of Dowsers
and codirector of its school

"Atala Toy is one of the top energy workers. She doesn't just 'read it and repeat it'; she understands."

—Robert T. McKusick, biomagnetic researcher
and past president of the Life Force Chapters of Phoenix
and Tucson Globe Dowsers

"Atala Dorothy Toy gives you an energy road map through pictures, stories, and exercises. Team up with your inner guides and shift, perceive, and communicate with all that is. Be prepared to embark on a remarkable journey that will open you up to a richer and fuller life as you connect and communicate with energies that affect you and world consciousness."

—Nancy Grace Marder,
executive director of Infinity Foundation

"Atala shows that our environment contains a host of spirits, fairies, devas, thought forms, and more. With a shift in perception and the help of inner guides, we can communicate with them and help resolve interdimensional issues. She makes us want to grab a camera for a long walk in the woods."

—Guy Spiro, past publisher of the *Monthly Aspectarian*,
Author of *Astro-Weather*